Beckoning

Poetry of Life

First Reviews - Extracts

Literary Arts Review, 13 January 2016

I wish Edward G. Bottomley had been publishing poetry for years, but it takes a lot of life experience for a writer to produce Beckoning. It is an insightful collection of poems about various aspects of Life, its phases and transitions, sadness and joys. It's sometimes witty, sometimes challenging, and as the title implies, beckons you to ponder the meaning of life and truly live it.

Born in northern England, Bottomley's career path includes both accountancy and photography. His combination of orderly thinking and creativity is reflected in Beckoning, where I found beautiful black-and-white photography sprinkled here and there between the imaginative, carefully crafted poems.

Beckoning is arranged into nineteen chapters of related content, with subjects such as Family, Arts, Humor, Values and Death. Each of the nearly two hundred poems can stand alone, with something of interest for everyone. The collection is largely nonfiction with three personal poems included: Shaping the Author, At Peace with One's Own Death and Taking a Ride. I was given a copy by the author in exchange for an honest review. I recommend that you add Beckoning to your bookshelf or Kindle.

Amazon UK (4) & US (3)
I love the mixture of honesty
Keep this anthology handy at all times – there are poems for everyone and all occasions. I love the mixture of honesty, insight, intellectual brilliance and controversy
One of the most surprising books of the year
I'm not sure I've read anything like it before with its eclectic mixture of poems that can cheer and please, comfort and inspire. I've been reading a few every morning with my cup of tea, engendering a small oasis of thought stimulation each day. Highly recommended.
Well worth the read!
A very thought provoking book of poetry. Everyone will find a poem that they can relate to.
Provides much food for thought & is very entertaining.
It explores personal, social & political aspects, as well as the meaning of life.
A call to embrace the challenges and joys of life...
The title, "Beckoning", could not be more appropriate as his prose compels us to explore and enjoy life's many adventures and unexpected twists and turns, while being fully mindful of the things we would usually rather not think about: the often painful challenges we all must face.
Odyssey of an Inquiring Mind
I'd say that most people at some point in their lives have thought about the purpose and meaning of life. Unfortunately few people take the time to articulate those thoughts and still fewer have the skill and acumen to describe them in verse.
This beckons!
Finally, a book of poetry with great depth!!

The full reviews can be found at: LiteraryArtsReview.com
Amazon Books UK
Amazon Books

Beckoning

Poetry of Life

Edward Bottomley

For Imogen, Thomas and Charlotte

The Aspiring Artist
The Vibrant Guitar
Coco and Poppy

Contents

Acknowledgements

It is difficult to know where to start and finish when considering acknowledgements.

Here goes!

Firstly, thanks to my very good friend, Lionel, in England. I talked to him, early in 2015, about my idea, of writing poetry, relating to my six proposed novels. As a result, he suggested I should put my books on hold and concentrate on writing the poetry. As he put it, the poetry would contain the essence of my thinking. After significant reflection I was persuaded and embarked, with a passion, on the journey. You have the results 'in your hands'.

Thanks to all those who suggested or inspired a poem not included in my original list - Ashley and Dennis in Arizona, Emi and Spencer in Chihuahua, Mexico, Duncan and Lionel in England, Natha in Mississippi and Chuck in New Mexico.

Closer to home, in Cochise County, thanks to all those you who have allowed me to indulge in 'testing the market' or given me some form of encouragement. I have bent the ears of Dave & Midge (frequently), Linda & Bill, Mark & Linda and Ken (an author of good standing). Support has come from Charlie & Claudia and Nancy.

Further afield, in Florida, encouragement has been received from Marion and, in Texas, from Jean and Bob. The inspiration I have found in Terlingua, Texas, has been amazing. People like Mimi, Jana and Jon (he of ugly vehicle fame) have been part of my evolution; as have the musicians who perform there, especially Ashley from Austin. I must mention Natha, again, in Mississippi - hours long poetry readings, over the telephone - with a shot (or two) of tequila :-), Bob & Carol Ann in Gonzaga Bay, Tony, Tony & Jim at Don Eddies, Tereso & Martha at Rancho Maria Teresa, all in Baja California. In France there is Bernard, my author friend. In England, Paul & Pauline and Peter & Pauline have teased me in encouraging ways.

There must be others, unnamed, who should pounce on me! As a self-publisher, editing is not a major problem ;-)

I couldn't finish without acknowledging and thanking my two daughters, Jill and Sarah in England, and their husbands Duncan and Michael. Thank you so much for your patience with my regular poetry refrain. Love you all!

Introduction

When I was seventeen I experienced the most profound year of my life. As a result, I have sought and continue to seek the meaning of life. Having exceeded religion's three score years and ten, I have some insight - having lived a life. The inspiration for this series of poems arose from the series of six fictional novels I am writing. They all have my three grandchildren in mind; none of whom has yet reached their latter teens. The objective is the creation of life awareness, from youth onwards - as a prompt to the individual's own thoughts. Disagreement makes for healthy discussion, provided each respects the other's point of view. Life beckons and we should each be searching to add value to the lives of others, as well as our own.

In choosing the poetry subjects, I created a list of titles, relating to life. They were not ones I necessarily wanted to write about, but ones I considered important. They are written with a view to highlighting different points of view and displaying some empathy for them.

I have indulged in including three personal poems - **Shaping the Author, At Peace with One's Own Death** and **Taking a Ride.** Also included, are three poems written specifically for my three grandchildren; with subjects of their choosing. They were written in February 2015 and are listed in the dedication.

I have taken a degree of liberty with the grammar for 'the sake of flow'. A few poems are conversations between two people and include *italics* for one of the characters.

The book does not need to be read, cover to cover, at one sitting. Rather, each poem is a discrete entity, capable of being read, and reread, in isolation. The chapters are organized by related content. The order of the poems could be changed to suit a variety of tastes or preferences. I have tried to cover many aspects of life but I'm aware there are subjects I have not included. There may be others I have mistakenly omitted. I am open to suggestions and may, from time to time, write an additional poem. Such poems will be freely available through Twitter. You can contact me there, at @EdwardReLife, should you wish to suggest an additional topic; or if you have a question or comment to make.

Two Opening Poems
1. Poetry   *A challenge*

Poetry

In general terms, what is this subject?
One which many easily reject
As you read these lines, do you have an open mind
Or are you struggling against a conviction of a negative kind?

Why not move, put the book back on the shelf
Why practice masochism on yourself
Maybe you have a tablet in your hand
Flick the switch, no further interest to be fanned

There are a few more lines you may care to read,
Before carrying out such a fateful deed
Briefly consider the last verse,
As the pros and cons you rehearse

To each a life is given,
Which many, to improve, have striven
Poetry with purpose, to dip in and out of,
Or a slight chance, of being like a pig, with a trough

On the fly
Think or don't buy
Hello or goodbye?

2. Shaping the Author   *Mental attitudes*

Shaping the Author

One should not underestimate the benefit of a stable home situation
Where, safely, you are free to grow and develop - a positive equation
Encouraged by caring parents to participate in activities and organizations
Choirboy, scouting, cycling, photography, chess - impactful occupations

By eleven, instilled with 'no such word as can't', by a teacher thundered
Then a boys' character-building school of 360, not the factory of 1100
At thirteen, a school trip to France, the start of becoming a Francophile
Church sermons twice every Sunday, from 8 to 14, shaped a values profile

My father's research work instilled what, when, where, how and why
Not a risk-taker, so my mother would articulate the adventurous cry
Through all the school years, a love of pure mathematics trained my mind
In latter ones, aspects of philosophy and psychology became intertwined

The consequence led me to where I found myself, at age seventeen
The crux of the matter was its culmination in a head to head clash, unseen
Mind games, every night, pitting religion against logic, strategy or tactics
An ongoing high level discussion with myself, on a par with didactics

The result, a win for logic; becoming part of being, forever onwards
It turned out to be part of molding my life and giving direction upwards
Soon afterwards, "What's money, unless you don't have any?" struck home
It was something my father said - away from its meaning I never did roam

Early twenties, a qualified Chartered Accountant, in an office, professional
Then the Certificate in Management Information and a concept obsessional
Maslow's hierarchy of needs led to a search for intellectual satisfaction
It was something I strongly believed in, giving my entire future traction

In my twenties, in an industrial manufacturing environment - a wise sage
The Factory Manager, thirty years my senior, with whom I did engage
Every month a need to meet; afterwards, discussions philosophical
Inspiration and the words "What's life if it's not challenges?" - so graphical!

Parallel with work, becoming deeply involved in politics, made one think
An abrupt end at twenty nine, when, from my conscience, I did not shrink
A three line whip, to tow the party line, something, sometimes, to decline
Towards being an all or nothing person I discovered I did incline

All this helps to explain my emphasis on values, truth and quality of life
Mental richness, more important than in the pocket - avoiding mental strife
Conceptual and critical thought, adventure, risk, never meeting a stranger
These underscore my poetry; activities occasionally exposing me to danger.

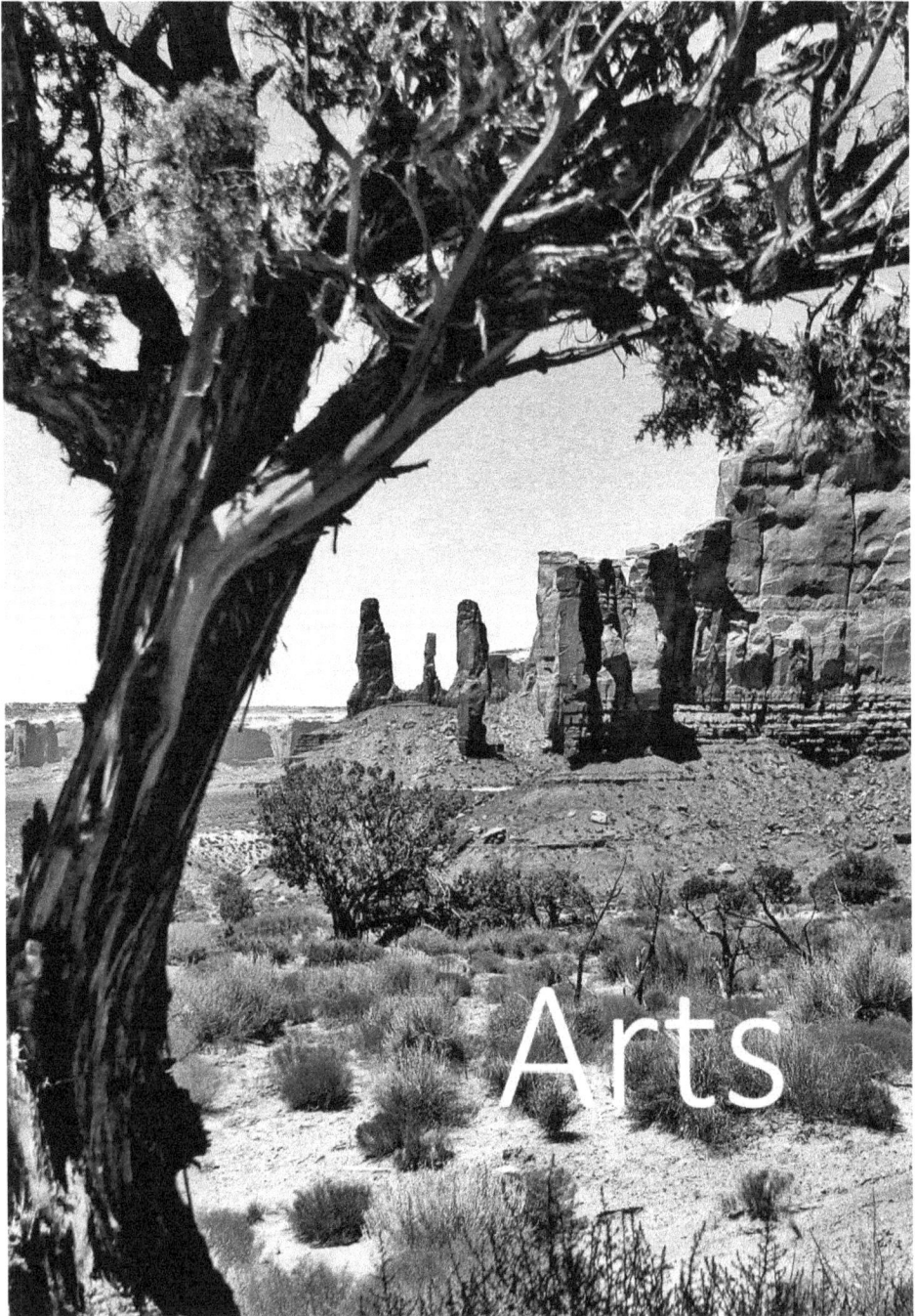

Arts

Beckoning [4] Arts

Arts

An artist's palette, a composer's notation sheets or a potter's clay
When they are put to good use, what is the creator hoping to portray?
To turn the mind, influence one's mood or transfix, with beauty hued
Hidden meanings, from your imagination, you should never try to exclude

Ask a question, make a statement, stir the emotions or provide eye candy
There are many explanations which can come in handy
There's a division between those which are visual and those performing
Either way, the best are to no pre-conceived ideas conforming.

Let's move on, from origination to interpretation,
To the realms of song and dance; and the stimulation of improvisation
An escape for some, who discover peace and relaxation,
Beyond, to connections with the soul, demanding explanation

There's a continuum bridging art and science.
Beautiful structures fulfilling the practical and of the ugly in defiance
Conceptual applications elevating the nature of humankind,
Leaving the ordinary far behind

However, it only needs a little thought to realize it doesn't finish there.
With a degree of effort, we can all make these things less rare
The art of conversation and the interiors of our homes are not impossible
Most important, sensory stimulation and belief in the art of the possible.

The Aspiring Artist

A feeling heart and a lively mind, combined
Went in search of inspiration to find
Creativity of a special or even unique kind,
The more normal or average to leave behind

A school of thought or a school of art
What would be the best way to play your part?
To run with the crowd or with individuality to stand out
To progress to certainty and get rid of the doubt

Constable, Gainsborough and Turner were painters romantic
Not for them the creation of scenes frantic
From Canaletto in Italy to Picasso in Spain
From studying these artists what would one gain

The stroke of a brush; the slide of a blade
For one's work to be paid, on the way to one's reputation being made
To rise to a challenge, to discover a passion
Qualities such as these will never go out of fashion

Make no mistake when appreciating L.S. Lowry
A world apart from Salvador Dali
For Rene Magritte, a painting of a pipe was not a pipe
And the modernism of Georgia O'Keeffe was of another type

In the world of pop art there's Warhol, Lichtenstein and Blek le Rat
Some who I know are very fond of that
So where should one go and what should one do
From which type of art will you take your cue?

The Beauty of Mathematics

Thinking of mathematics - do you see difficulty or topics displeasing
Does the subject leave you cold; and near to freezing
Or could there be a glimmer of hope and an angle worth seizing?
If so, great - we could conceivably try a little paradoxical teasing

A good place to start may be to think of poetry and art
They have fine meter and perspective which could play a useful part
From there to rhythms and beats of music; and sounds of spicy chords
There's something producing harmony, without the pain of discords

Turning to dance, it's the movements which count
Like the rotational symmetry of flamenco, two dancers mount
Not always, but often in nature, it's Fibonacci's numbers having a huge say
Petals of flowers, spirals in shells, even the branches of trees falling prey

The Golden Ratio and Golden Spiral could be mentioned in the same gasp
Parthenon, Pyramids, DNA, hurricanes and spiral galaxies within grasp
The Möbius band and the Klein bottle are wonders of topology
With these and more, an interest in mathematics never needs an apology!

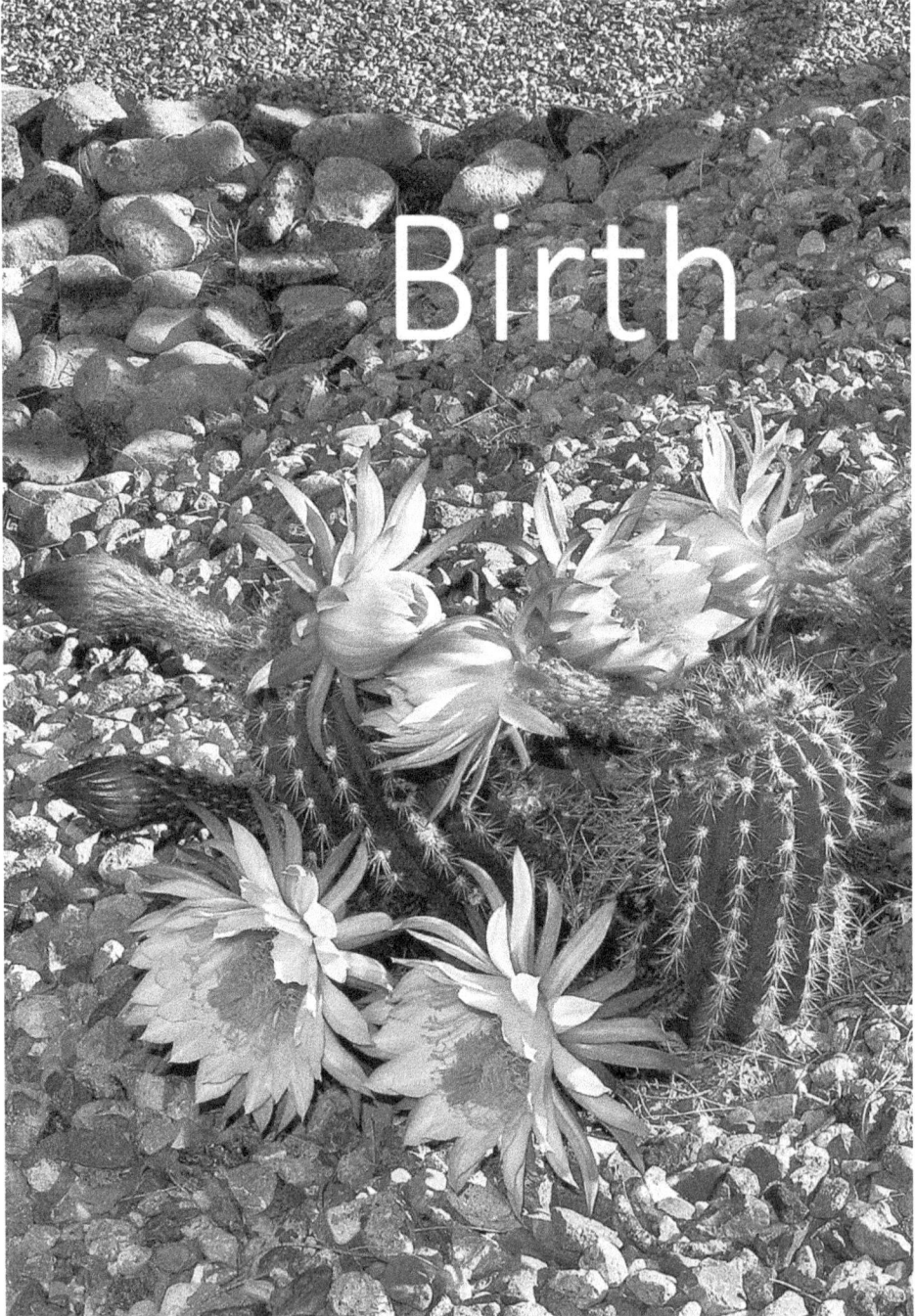

Birth

Birthing Business

It begins; it will end, but who knows how it will conclude?
In the widest sense there are many possibilities to include
Physical, mental; a preference to dictate or be treated gentle
What type was it, is it or will it be; maybe even experimental
Fluctuation, anticipation, even provocation
Easy, routine, difficult
Forced, predetermined, spontaneous
Varied criteria, yet evolution is a must
From A to Z in one, it cannot be
Creations, in every form, have features in common
From commencement to conclusion, different stages, in profusion
Deep in space, deep in the womb, deep in the mind
At some point a definitive action leading to some gain in traction
Growth becoming essential - as a matter existential.

Pregnancy

'To have or not to have?' is the question needing a decision
For some it may depend upon their religion
For those of a more secular incline
It could be a question of "by accident or design?"

For many, important aspects are of avoiding errors
Or of procreation of a new generation - like reflections in mirrors
The issue of money should sometimes be a wiser influence
But, in a heated moment, an imperative confluence

Perhaps, for most, it's the natural thing to do
And there can be such a huge strength in family glue
For some, continuity may reign supreme
For those less fortunate, it may remain nothing but a dream

Once the discovery has been confirmed, the journey starts for real
Not only for the mother-to-be; it's vital the father be in on the deal
To one partner, some aspects come naturally and can seem obvious
For the other, at first, oblivious, but hopefully not impervious

Communication and understanding enhance the exciting experience
One of mutual discovery - at times, entailing resilience
Lots of dos and don'ts impact both sides of the equation
It takes skill and possibly guidance to minimize abrasion

Even with unexpected complications, this is a shared chapter
As partners they must each accept responsibility for a common captor
Unexpressed or unrealistic expectations, left pending, are divisive
Two-way conversations with purpose; positive and not derisive

When these aspects are properly addressed it's like a transformation
The delights of your special relationship receiving affirmation
Pleasure from planning for the new arrival, much more than pure survival
A togetherness, in anticipation of becoming a family, has no rival

Nevertheless, as the day gets nearer, impatience can start to take hold
Despite the expectant parent classes for which you'd both enrolled
Questions about the date - early, on time or late can cause debate
Last minute concerns about the delivery will not necessarily elate

The end will come; there is no avoidance, yet with complete escape
There will be exertion and there could be problems; maybe red tape
The finale will grant resolution; it will have all been so worthwhile
Life, new warmth in loving arms, a new family - a gift, a smile.

Miscarriage

Warning signs or out of the blue
When it happens it is so unfortunate, yet unavoidably true
No satisfaction; more a mother's sense of being alone with the loss
A feeling of defeat, like bearing a cross

The timing may have been early or late
But a life has been lost and such is not open to debate
This is not about people, with an alternative view, shaking the tree
It's about parents-to-be, who did not wish to be set free

How do they cope and what do they do?
Without having had the experience, it can be easy for me; and for you
If it happens early on, some parents may take it in their stride
For others, especially with beliefs, it may be a very challenging ride

The later it happens the more difficult it becomes
Any tendency to optimism can be an emotion it numbs
It could make a difference being a first or subsequent child
But, nevertheless, one has to find a way to stop being riled

One needs to have exposure to some form of closure
An unlikely find in any form of brochure
Comfort can be found in a healthy medical report
And also, through family and friends, giving their support

Life progresses from day to day
And, gradually, the future comes back into play
The couple starts to find themselves on the way to recovery
And the cherry on the cake will be an exciting discovery.

Abortion

Minds with common purpose, in union of the flesh
Conception of an idea from an angle - fresh
Stages developmental; hoping for nothing detrimental
Will they be for real or only prove experimental

Success or failure in varying degrees
Occasional resulting actions, in certain specific quarters, may displease
Disappointment may have been the order of the day
For others, new laws may be how they get their way

Often, things go to plan; less frequently a mishap may transpire
To call a halt may be wise and fulfill the participants' desire
Money, health, even life may be at stake
Who has the right to decide whether or not to apply the brake?

Chapter 11 has nothing on strong religious views
Yet these, and more, others may abuse
Always wrong or always right
Always exceptions needing an unfailing fight!

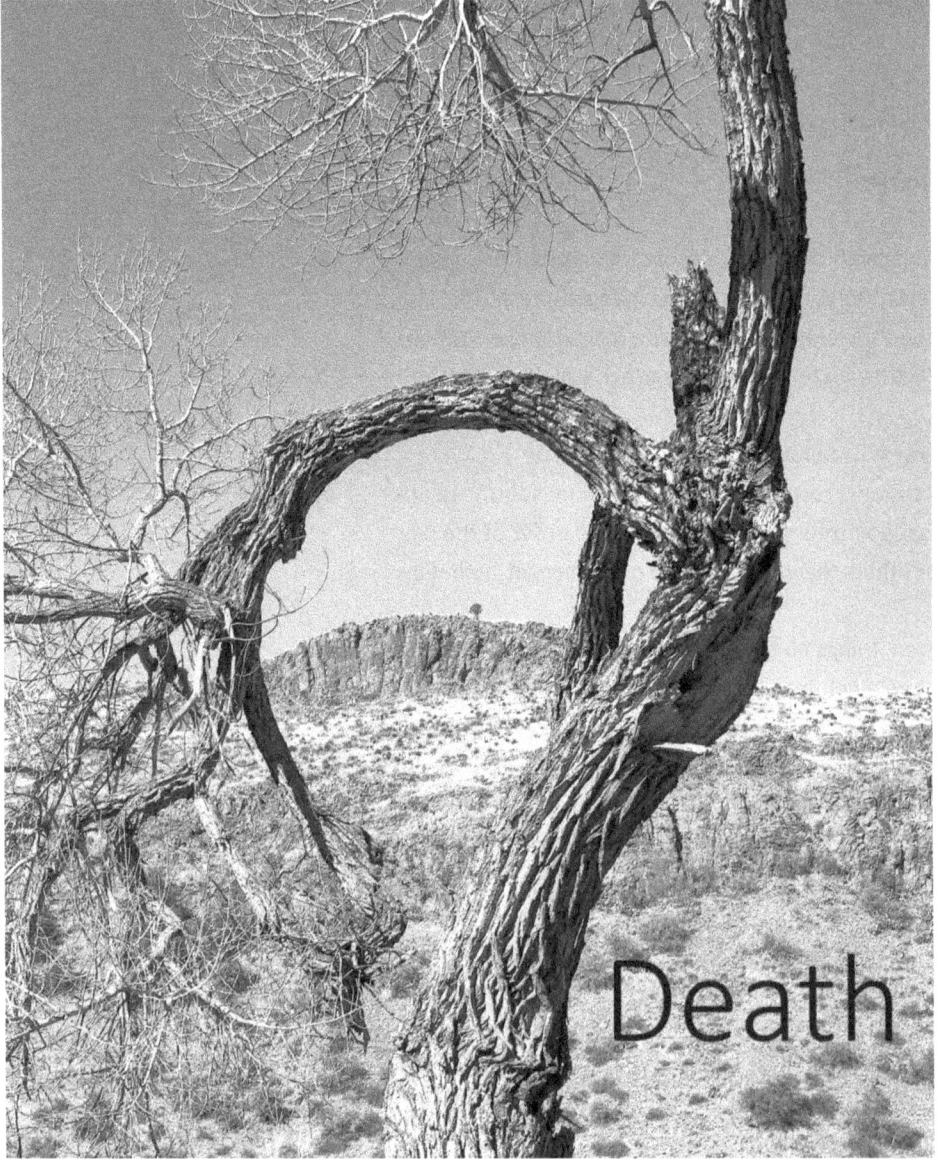

Beckoning [14] Death

Death

A difficult subject for consideration - in terms of everything involved
First, should we, in any way, from our own responsibility, be absolved?
Certain aspects, the law dictates - one's state of mind so unkind
It implies, to a delegated end, one might have to be resigned

Even so, this is life's last challenge, somehow sneaking up on us all
Whether in fact or in fiction, it seems its interest can never pall
Awareness increasing, as one crosses the line to less life left to live
Others will start their bucket lists, themselves, outstanding treats to give

Thought is needed to do the best for ourselves and those we leave behind
Things unfinished and plans for our demise need to be defined
The necessary willpower varies from person to person
But, without action, the pressure will surely worsen

There are wills, living wills and powers of attorney
DNR or not and burial or cremation raise queries about the journey
Thoughts of a meaningless existence, or of suicide, are extremely trying
Bigger questions, for society at large - euthanasia and assisted dying

One can fear, hope or dream about the circumstances of one's passing
Better to plan and then be free to continue, positive experiences, amassing
Some dignity, as one passes the baton, is what one aims to orchestrate
With comfort in then being able, on one's remaining future, to concentrate.

At Peace with One's Own Death

The moment would be here all too soon
Would it really be the case
Did one need time to expand
Expand on what?

Expand on what had or might have been
Expand the time available for goodbyes
Expand one's understanding of what life had been all about
And would still be about, for those one would shortly leave behind

What about aspects of fear
They might play large when the end is so near
Put them aside or take them in one's stride
At the final moment, one can only, in one's passing hide

Then to the question of regrets
Maybe a degree of sorrow about a few things one never forgets
Regrets, things one wishes one could undo or change
No, those are definitely out of range

There is comfort and a sense of peace
A sense of living on in certain ways
Hopefully one leaves behind genes, thoughts or influences on mankind
Little things which would never have been and special people never seen

As the curtain comes down on the final act
One hopes one has had some kind of impact
But, regardless, peace and comfort line one's cask
My satisfaction, with my own life, is more than I ever dared to ask

I think of family and of friends - those loved and loved in return
I think of Yorkshire, Texas, Arizona and Mexico for which I did yearn
The pride and the pleasure, despite life's ups and downs
All these envelop me and I have the best of crowns.

Beckoning [16] Death

Drugs

Beckoning [17] Drugs

Drugs and Influences

Drugs of the body and drugs of the mind
Sometimes both - deceitfully combined
What it is about the human race
Causing us to allow such influences to invade our space
What is a drug and how can it be defined

Can there ever be a clear line
Between those for good and those which many would malign
Ignorance is bliss
Never had, never miss
Profit motives lead astray, by design

How do adventure and risk come into play?
What diverts a person the wrong way?
Inner responsibility or outer control
Can every individual always be on patrol?
Pain, pleasure, hope, despair, many more will have their say

What is the damage and the opportunity cost
Benefits abound, so not all is lost
What are the pros and cons of legalization?
Those will vary from nation to nation
The law of the jungle, the law of the land - never to be crossed

To control or be controlled
To which side of the fence might you be cajoled?
Are you in favor or are you against
And, don't forget the border, still being fenced
Demanding many more assets to be effectively patrolled

Where does the responsibility lie?
Why would any individual desire such an induced high
Lack of discipline, lack of restraint, hastening one's demise
In a manner impossible to surmise
Such may be the way to be left to hang out to dry.

Drug Wars

Drug wars; wars against drugs
Drug wars; thugs against thugs
Wars against drugs; saving souls from deep holes
Drug wars; finding an unexpected head which rolls
Drugs; hardly the subject of kisses and hugs

There is no easy answer, there is no sudden fix
Authorities and do-gooders, in bed, what a mix
Power and psychology, aimed at friend and foe alike
If you don't accept it, you might want to take a hike
Dare to follow the money to the source of the tricks.

Family

Marriage

Words flowed, embers flared; though winter, no need for a blaze
Gone was the bubbling enthusiasm of their earlier days
Relaxed feelings of warmth and coziness, as they reminisced
Nothing's perfect; ups and downs had been part of the grist

They felt so fortunate, compared with most of whom they'd heard
Over their life together, there was nothing they would have preferred
A oneness had been portrayed, when they took their wedding vows
Now they understood it and its value they did espouse

"Do you remember when we discussed giving up freedom for a family?"
"We certainly got that one right." replied the grandmother, dreamily
"It's added so much value to our life experience, as one."
"Children and grandchildren, such extra meaning, and they'll live on."

"We've shared such a lot and had an amazing partnership."
"Times have changed, marriage now signifying uncertain membership."
"I can live with it; but truly better with a new and different word."
"Like two of a kind becoming 'glarried' - too absurd?"

Baby Manifestations and Early Childhood

It's so easy to witness crying, eating and sleeping - not to mention pooping
A new and amazing creation, a unique person who encourages snooping
Much learning going on, especially for your warm, cuddly bundle of joy
For first-time parents, how to care and react; and the techniques to employ?

Time passes, stages reached, progressive indications being so important
We've read books, talked to specialists, family and friends - expectant
Before we get too deep, let's think instead of simple pleasures
Like first smiles and coordinated eye movements - things one treasures

Some things vary from mother to mother, as a tiny mouth sucks and grows
And it doesn't take long, before there's a need for a new size of clothes
Do you remember the first little squeeze of your finger?
It's one of those things which I'm sure, will forever linger

Despite delights, a need to be observant for signs which may be missing
They may be unlikely, but not the subject of reluctant acquiescing
Over the months, signs of communication and advances in movements
It may be difficult to tell whether they are meant to encourage inducements

Probably many broken nights, almost resulting in occasional fights
Hopefully, all more than counterbalanced by enthralling human insights
As the first year goes by, new family patterns have been established
Practice makes perfect and, despite the unexpected, routines polished

Transitions - newborn, infant to toddler; first birthday's been and gone
From inaction to great mobility; more necessity to keep one's eye on
A new personality taking shape, trying, on occasion, its parents to ape
A time when, from the idea of a brother or sister, there may be no escape

The second year is so unlike the first, with words becoming more related
Vaccinations progress towards completion; curiosity continues unabated
Boisterousness, tantrums, bursting into tears and looks you can't refuse
But don't let the idea, of the terrible two's, give you the blues.

Parenthood

A flower bloomed and spread its seed - a new generation to be conceived
A bird laid eggs in its nest, built in a safe place it had secretly perceived
All living things - driven by the urge to survive and propagate
Humanity is no exception; but different features we demonstrate

People go beyond innate desire and the variety of ways of making love
To be parents or not to be; for some, with guidance from above
Becoming a father without desire or, worse, a mother-to-be lamentably
These are not things being as they should be; nor do they sit comfortably

There is an ongoing responsibility, which should not be untaken lightly
A commitment requiring compatibility; an urge to look forward, brightly
It all sounds rather challenging and, indeed, it is; but not to be forsaken
Like so many things in life, it necessitates self-belief in a route unmistaken

The rewards should be so much greater than the bumps along the way
Varied tendencies will be on display; at times like performers in a cabaret
Despite the worries and frustrations there is so much joy to behold
From innocence and developing personality to individuality uncontrolled

It doesn't stop at age eighteen or at the magical milestone of twenty-one
It evolves in fulfilling ways, long after, from the family home, they've gone
Its foundation lies in the nature of giving and of concern for others
It's not purely the urge to reproduce and live on by proxy or to be mothers

Education, values, opportunities, citizenship all within a loving embrace
Yet not one of absolute control for there's a need to give children space
They need to develop, grow and be guided on the road to independence
Evolving into best friends and parents - a new cycle of transcendence.

Family Matrices

Thinking about blood relationships, do you find a measure of perplexity
Are you treading a slope towards more generations and complexity
Possibly cascading up or down; wearing a smile or burdened by a frown
Do you believe you could drown or picture yourself wearing a crown?

Such concerns, not only for you and me, but for everyone on the planet
All rubbing shoulders, like arils in a mega pomegranate
From babe in the woods, to being over the hill
There is no escape, unlike the option of taking a pill

Yet, there is so much truth in blood being thicker than water
Regardless of whether talking about parents; or a son or a daughter
Life is full of challenges and one can need people on whom one can count
There may be a few real friends; but support from family is paramount

So, as you squabble with sibling rivalries or wish for one you never had
Remember, what should be the essential value of a family launching pad
Loving arms, a shoulder to cry on - someone you can call or lean on
If everything else is taken away, who else will there be to rely on?

Generations

Wrinkle-furrowed brow with age and weather worn
Gray hair, uncropped, receded - almost bald
Spectacles adorn, heavy as the nose
This pillar of a family, a man with craggy jaw
Seated, rocking in a corner, curtains not yet drawn
Upon his baggy trousers, heavy belt loosely buckled,
A small child moves, pulls at his open collar, says
'Grandpa, what's the game?'
No words were forthcoming
Just the changes in the eyes
The spreading of the skin as
With look delighted, and taking him in his arms
A simple pleasure, deeply felt - warm, enveloping.

Pets

There are many guises; no prizes for guessing those most frequent
In caring hands the benefits of ownership flow, typically consequent
Smiling faces, relaxed minds; therapies of various kinds
So much benefit to children and the elderly - like special finds

They are good for health in many ways, not least in keeping fit
A great antidote to loneliness, as I'm sure many would admit
Dogs, cats and horses most commonly fill this space
They are all so domesticated and relate well to the human race

What about others - ones which may be exotic or truly unexpected
Tarantulas, scorpions, spiders or snakes - unlikely to be selected
For a minority, the opposite is the case, and there are a few around
With proper care, tolerance of differences can create common ground

Of course there is a rider, no matter the species or its compatibility
To those who would consider ownership, it comes with responsibility
Displaying genuine attention and affection for those in one's charge
Will brings its rewards and an aspect of your life it will enlarge.

Coco and Poppy

In a home, not far from a pond,
Lived two rabbits of which Charlotte was fond
They were both lop-eared, with hearing aids floppy
One was called Coco and the other named Poppy

Coco arrived with a warning - a territorial male
But happy to share his space with a friendly female
They might have been named Hoppity and Floppity
But such names wouldn't have been very lop-witty

Although they lived in a cage
They were never seen in a rage
Sometimes having the run of the house
They used their wits and knew not to grouse

Hopping and jumping, their claws they could harden
Especially with their tube and quarters in the garden
Trimming their nails was something they hated
It had to be done and so was never debated

Coco was larger and Poppy a little smaller
They liked to be held, even by a new caller
There were plenty of things they liked to touch
But they could always return, to cuddle in their hutch.

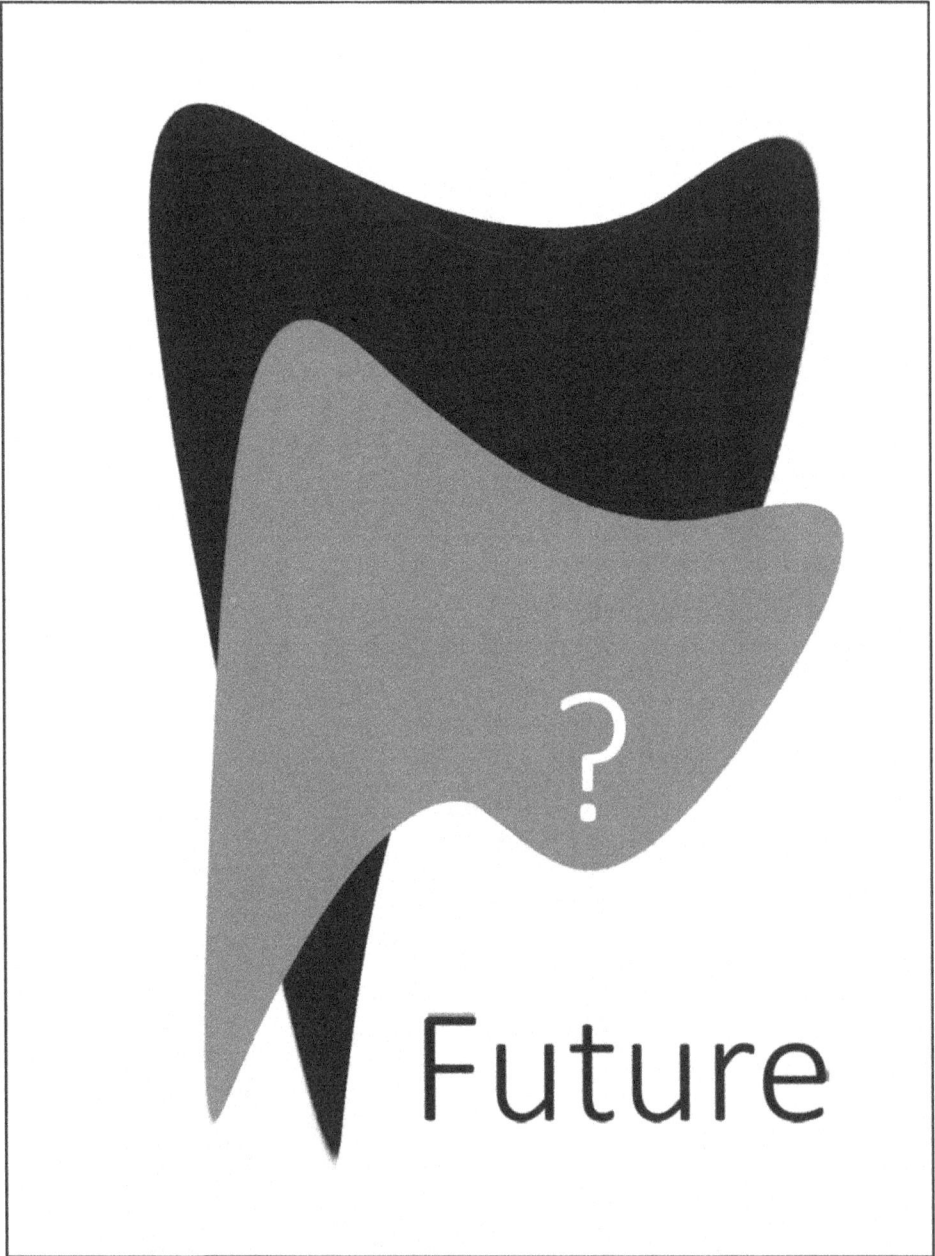

? Future

Beckoning [28] - Future

Future - The Concept

When your mind wanders, where does it go? Does it leave today behind?
How does it work as it pursues the unknown, beyond, to find?
Influences of imagination and reality - fencing and dancing
A balance one seeks to redress, like an infection needing lancing
Relativity is at play again - pleasure for one, for another, pain
Not only humanity but nature and cosmology share the driving lane
What timescales do they each consider, in toiling remorselessly to deliver?
Vessels, of all shapes and sizes, jostling in a crowded river
The flow of time, uncontrolled, with hugely different perspectives
Can lead to the use of unusually provocative invectives
Regardless of disagreement the process will not wait
Whatever the rights and wrongs change will still emanate
Fear not where it will take you, you're not the last in the queue
Whatever you think and wish there is no certainty it will come true.

Future - Angles for the Individual

Who knows how many years are ahead; and how they can be foretold
Do you know or would you rather rely on a fortuneteller, bold
I'm sure neither is true and you'd rather, of your own life, take hold
We're not fully in charge, but don't want to be left out in the cold

Of course these things vary very much, depending upon one's age
Do we have a measuring gauge, as each new day turns a page?
As we grow and develop, throughout our seemingly endless schooldays
At what point do we seek to have some influence, within the maze?

There is a need to dream and aim for the moon
In some ways, maybe success can't come too soon
Still, plans and patience can be more important than harebrain schemes
And is one better solo or as part of fulfilling teams?

Lessons, learned from mistakes we make,
Help improve the ingredients to bake a better cake
However, sometimes it can be difficult to recover from a bitter blow
Especially if some thoughtless person tells you 'I told you so'

Yet, there is no way out and one has to continue on the road
It's presumably very evident - how one reaps, from the seeds one sowed
Relationships, beyond question, are important at such a stage
They influence your direction and your thoughts they engage

It's clear by now; it's not just about you, but others too
All sorts of components bound together by your evolutionary glue
Ambitions fulfilled or maybe too late to be realized
But hopes still needed, in order to avoid being marginalized

For you there may be a way, via your children or by way of theirs
Which will do so much to alleviate your cares
It helps, to move forward, when you have a passion or fulfill a need
Each will provide an aim, facilitating your ability to proceed

There is an interesting conceptual facet to all of this
To conclude without mentioning it would be awfully remiss
There is no time like the present, looking ahead is a matter of conjecture
Now is now and, no matter how hard one tries, will never be the future.

Beckoning [31] - Future

Future - In Totality

In aspiring to completeness and consideration of the whole
One commits to undertaking the achievement of an extraordinary goal
The cosmos, nature and humankind combined - asking to be defined
From everything we know, to extrapolate; three stars to be aligned

Most will say, such an ambition is an impossibility; not worth the struggle
How on earth could it be achieved? Such divergent equations to juggle
For many, selfishly, it is because they don't wish to be involved
They'd rather carry on as they are; from responsibility absolved

Nevertheless, a lead has to come from somewhere; whoever may dare
Do you want to sit back, despite knowing, acting as though unaware?
Air is polluted, oceans and seas enhanced by sewage and plastic, floating
Hearing these words do you sit in front of your grandchildren, gloating?

The effects of global warming and climate change, whatever the cause,
Should be built into our calculations; if necessary enacted by laws
Although they affect so many nations, achieving a common front
Is not possible without building much more trust, which is being blunt

Cosmic forces continue to create effects, with no respect for their subjects
Nature has ways of coming on strong, turning people into foreign objects
Maybe we have to go with the flow and, unlike Canute, not fight the tides
Finding guides, to help resolve the interests which the world divides

The geography of one's birth is not something to be the focus of scorn
It's part of what molds everyone; its loss could cause one to mourn
People are renewable, unlike many of the world's natural supplies
Overall, the interrelationships, we cannot disguise, unless we're unwise.

Future - Mankind

The word represents a totality, masking a multitude of smaller parts
Consideration of the benefit, to the whole, is where our thinking starts
By definition, it must mean compromise; not to everyone's taste
To do otherwise increases the disparity, lives to waste

If we had a compass it would help in reaching our destination
How can we define it and do away with procrastination
I've used it before, 'enlightened self-interest', and may do so again
It precipitates action, before consequences cause too much pain

We talk of superstitions and sometimes things coming in threes
Food, water and energy; challenges which could trigger a squeeze
Some may, rightly, ask about health, education and the economy
Justifiable concerns influencing every individual's autonomy

Single-mindedness, for any purpose, usually leads to excess
Those, with the most, need to consider acquiescing to special largesse
The problem is often one of timescale or alternative perspective
With so many cultures around the world, action has been defective

Benefits from man-made resources, robotics and other technology
Provide help, but are neither complete solutions nor pure apology
Leadership and sacrifice, coupled with initiative and moral support
Mankind, in all its glory, to a better equilibrium must transport.

Future - Cascading Down

From the infinite cosmos to the multitude, making up the Milky Way,
More celestial bodies, in our sky, than people on the earth today
So many with challenges; but still harboring dreams and aspirations
For those more fortunate - achievable; for billions - bad vibrations

Support has been forthcoming and there will be more for dire situations
However, there are limitations, giving rise to failure to meet expectations
Some, who believe in competition and Darwin's approach to survival,
Will never take us towards the trail of human dignity revival

It's all very well having augmented reality, crypto currencies and drones
But progress could be directed towards turning less exciting stones
The battles, between religion and secularism or cultural traditions
Highlight how essential it is to reconcile positions and effect transitions

To say these things are impossible, so why bother to try
Masks selfishness, comfort zone mentalities and other fish to fry
The battles for power and domination veer towards abomination
Redirected to the least fortunate could avoid long-term ruination.

Invention

"Necessity is the mother of invention"; words with tenuous links to Plato
Whether it is true or not may be something of a hot potato
Fast forward to the twenty-first century and transformations substantial
So many driven by inspiration, not necessarily for reasons purely financial

The past is the past and the necessities of the future loom large
What sort of minds, and from where in the world, will lead the charge
Consider the fundamentals of food and water, for an expanding population
Inventiveness and ingenuity - vital parts of evolutionary correlation

Imagine more potable water produced from the world's seas and oceans
Flowing through pipes, like oil and gas, with equivalent motions
In terms of feeding earth's billions, who knows what should be predicted
With a rising cost of water - menu choices progressively restricted

The environment and global warming, including bee pollination,
Are fraught with argument, as possible causes of humanity's ruination
Consider natural resource limitations and specific types of pollution
The need is for solutions; not absolution or periodic revolution

To produce answers is not easy and needs significant creative thought
Initiating essential change cannot be over-emphasized and must be sought
Whilst new products, across the range of human life, may be amazing
It is resourcefulness, in achieving mental change, one should be praising.

Water

So precious, without it, there would be no existence
Yet, many places where inadequate supplies lower resistance
Oceans awash, with nothing to drink; dams whose levels continually sink
Neither is always true, but they still make you think

Actions, consequences, questions of population. Need more stimulation?
Perhaps you might consider the subject of reserve manipulation?
Solutions can be found, until one discovers one's self legally included
At which point, one's confidence may no longer be exuded

It's wonderful to be an optimist, when it's tempered with realism,
But, with life's ultimate basic, do you want to entrust it to capitalism
The alternatives are limited and will not appeal to one and all
Without unbiased controls, who knows what, in the future, might befall?

Health

→EMERGENCY

Beckoning [37] - Health

Use of Pills and Potions

Do you take none at all or enough to make you rattle
Are they an occasional help or is your life a complete battle
Necessary medications or, with optimism, supplements to health
Does cost concern you - taking a disproportionate share of your wealth?

Prescription, over the counter or with a need for things illicit
If you had to do without, how much would your body miss it?
Of course, it may be more than purely physical
And, regardless of the reason, may seem entirely logical.

Do you worry about side-effects or being administered combinations
If you do, have you any idea what would be the indications
The potential for variation could well be timescale dependent
Does your knowledge or experience provide the advantage of precedent?

When one gets down to essentials and getting on with one's life
Convenience is important, like cutting with a truly sharp knife
But the crux of the matter comes down to expertise
To obtaining the best advice and avoiding being down on your knees.

Health in the Balance

Recommendations of does and don'ts flow fast
Genes, at birth, mean, to some extent, the die is cast
When we are young, it's not even in our own hands
And think how other factors vary, across the world's many lands

One thing in common - we all have a mind and a body
Even someone with a name like Serena Oddy
I don't know whether a person with such a name exists, or not
If I met her, I would apologize on the spot

But, back to the interplay of the physical and mental
It's not as though we can go out and exchange a rental
How to make the best of what we've each got
Enhance the process before we finally rot

There's diet and exercise and help from the medical profession
Plus aspects of philosophy and humor of which we are in possession
Family, work and other relationships very much matter
And self-image may be the subject of a lot of internal chatter

There are ways in which we are all exposed to risk
Some we might find by doing a self-frisk
Searching for the right balance in the most important type of wealth
A life-long journey to optimize every stage of health.

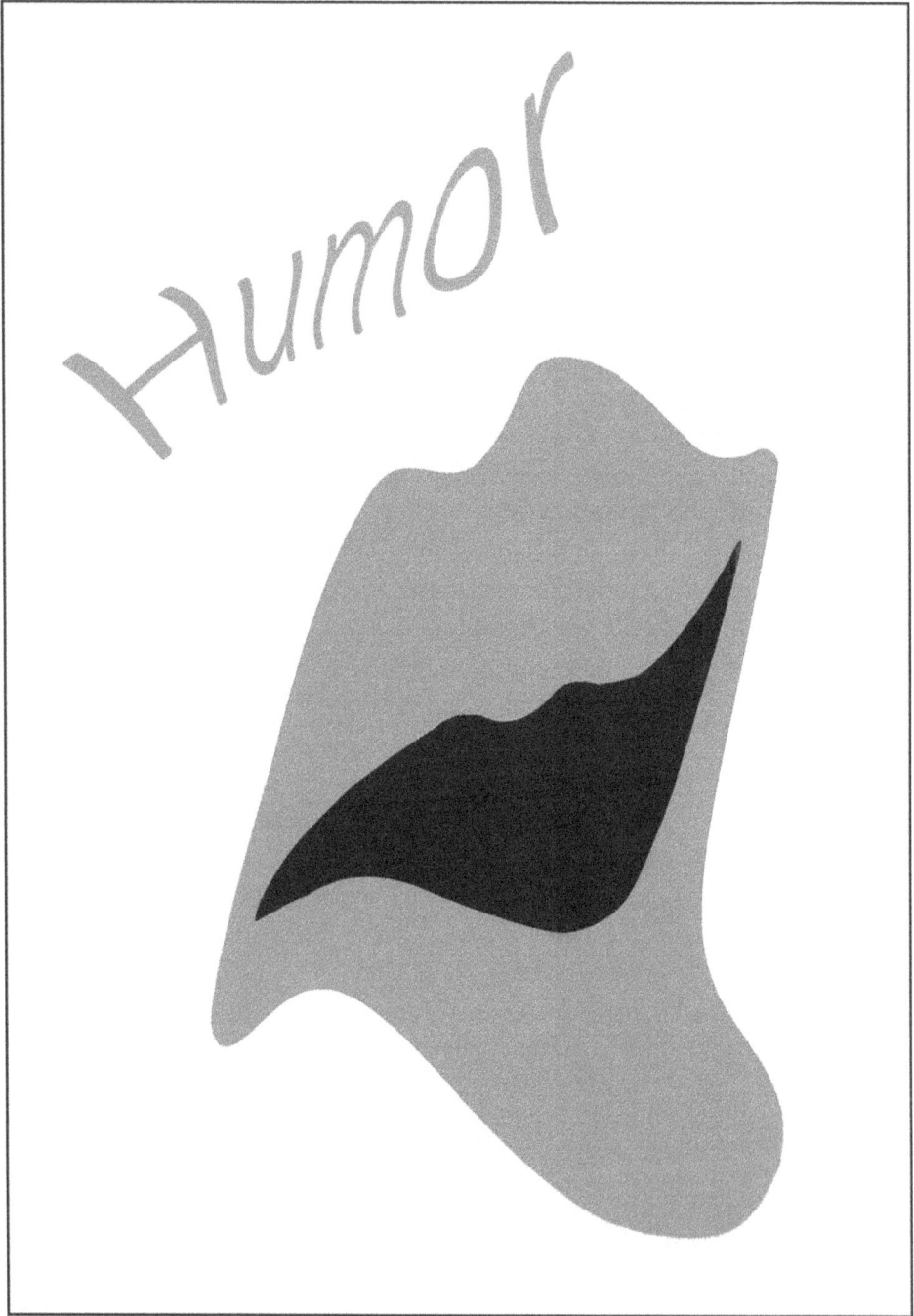

Beckoning [40] - Humor

Humor

When was the last time, at your own expense, you laughed?
Did it feel like an art or a craft or as though you were just plain daft
Were you purely lost in the moment or trying to escape disaster
As you flew over the handlebars - glad you hadn't been going even faster

Ever been killing yourself, with laughter, at another person's expense
Such is more likely to aggravate than restore a broken fence
Even so, it could be interpreted differently, according to circumstances
Especially, laughing with, not against, a friend who cavorts and dances

How do you develop a sense, of seeing the funny side, in young kids?
Above all, if it relates to something they know each parent forbids
Maybe you could use some silly words and dress them up as clowns
Then you could do the wrong thing, together, while searching for crowns

Instead, you might find other forms of inanity to bring tears to your eyes
Get the dopamine and endorphins flowing, never mind the disguise
You could lift your mood and detect a better feeling of well-being
As you gaze through a telescope and experience being all-seeing

Perhaps hard to believe, but problems at work may be more readily solved
If it proves to be the case, from undue merriment you could be absolved
We can all benefit, at times, from not coating ourselves in grave solemnity
But don't get carried away, to the point of needing indemnity

There are many types and styles - from the best to the insulting or sarcastic
To indulge in the latter, appropriate on occasion, but often too drastic
Humor is one of the best qualities in life and great for stress management
Why not start anew, become a psychologist and make your own judgment.

Don't be Alone

I thought I was alone, as I cycled on a mountain trail, until
Looking down, I saw human and animal tracks, crossing, it gave me a chill
I wondered who they were and where they'd gone
It set my mind buzzing and gave me something to think on

The result was really, rather strange
As my destination came into range
It was all about pairs, linked in rhyme
They'd certainly helped to pass the time

Each was like a herd of two
You know, something like a pouch and a kangaroo
My mind had jumped to things complimentary - on the rebound
It was easy, to forgive and forget, until I got lost and then was found

I was off down another track, with a cheerful grin
It took me round twists and turns; through vegetation thick and thin
I wondered what would happen next, as it started going up and down
There were pros and cons to this type of ride, not a place to act the clown

I never saw a horse and carriage, or any signs of love and marriage
A choice between a rock and a hard place, for a rest, I did disparage
I'd had to choose between paths - right and wrong
The last thing I needed was search and rescue, my excursion to prolong

It all felt somewhat cloak and dagger but not exactly frightening
Returning, before dark, was touch and go, due to thunder and lightning
I'd felt like Jekyll and Hyde, coordinating body and soul, looking ashen
I didn't want to be deemed high and mighty; but with ambition and passion.

In a Spin

When you're in a whirl and meet yourself coming back
Have you ever thought you might be on the right track?
As you passed from one extreme to the other
Did you see one opposite as the converse's brother?

Let's try a little experiment by continuing to be contrary
We need care and can't pick a series of words arbitrary
Let's start on the left then move to the right
Turning to wrong hardly makes something suitable, but don't get uptight

Flick the switch of equivalence to fitting, before reversing into improper
Which wouldn't be honest, more like deceitful - we could come a cropper
Guileless could mirror guarded, taking us into open before close
Could we risk a step from there to start, before disembark?

We could get on this conveyor belt before we descend and follow the rise
Before our eyes, turn into slump, then grow and shrink - another guise
But let's move on; we don't want to retreat, such would be a defeat
So near, so let's remain. No, I've changed my mind - I'd rather we left!

Pass

One hundred and sixty kilometers at a maximum speed of eighty K
Remoteness, heading from Sonora to Chihuahua one day
Straight across plains, after meandering climbs through various hills, until
Amid the open vistas, grades and switchbacks, about which not to enthuse
Despite the nature of the inspiring views

A small Nissan sedan had been closing the gap, at speed
As though the driver had great reason for haste, indeed
Fortunately he was not quite on my tail
As, around the next steep corner, we were both fortunate
On my rear end he did not himself impale

Descending traffic of varied hue
Was headed up by two trucks in red and blue
Not nose to tail but side by side
As complete as the road was wide
The existence of a double yellow line totally denied
There was absolutely nowhere for me to hide

My right of way was in dispute
I had no time to think of anything remotely cute
My instincts told me to break before it was too late
There was no time, with myself, to have a debate
He was in the wrong, but I was not about to come on strong

One could have classed it as a miracle
There was no competition of things physical
Five drivers, each with a decision
Instantaneously correct, avoided a fateful collision

My abrupt halt brought the Nissan to a sudden stop
The red truck continued its steady downhill drop
As, just in time, a gap opened behind
A space, just right for the blue truck, was defined
Courtesy of a fifth driver who displayed a sharp sense of mind

Once more starting on my way
I noticed the Nissan was a shade of gray
Considerately, behind me it did stay
It seemed his need to rush had been curtailed
Maybe even his commonsense had prevailed

We continued our slow and risky climb
But he didn't, yet, speed up to me a second time
The road cutting through towering rock
Doubling as the ascent's crest and the end of Sonora by less than a block

Gravity and centrifugal force united to create the first Chihuahuan descent
Nissan man's patience not yet spent
Until at last the curves and gradient did relent
A glance in my mirror told me what it meant
A pent-up urge morphed into a surge, as on his way he went.

Life is Rife

When you think of life do you think of people
Or some sort of bird perched on a steeple?
Out in the desert, when there's a smell of skunk
You might want to hibernate and become a monk

If you ever wanted to follow a rat down a hole
You'd have to be as slim as a twisted pole
Then there are flowers, whose aromas have special powers
Or a giant redwood, which over the countryside towers

In the heart of the city you might consider yourself an ant
In the heat of the day, out on the trail, like a dog, you may need to pant
As for the snake in the grass, well, we'll let such a creature pass
And the thought of being a crab could fill you with thoughts, drab

In large parts of the world there are weeds everywhere
But there are also fields of crops and herds of animals, tended with care
Such variety, not to mention all those things living in the sea
Ever considered being a bee, making sweet honey, especially for me?

The Vibrant Guitar

Six in line adorned a body fine
Depth and character, like a wonderful wine
A complex of rich burgundy and brilliant white
The way it played was a unique sight

A dancing plectrum, with no need for hands
Produced tunes and rhythms from many lands
It danced to the Samba; felt sad with the Blues
On its feet it wore new pointed shoes

Its sounds flowed long and its fullness was strong
For its followers it could do no wrong
A Mexican sombrero it wore for a hat
It strummed jazz in New Orleans but still found time for a chat

With melodies Hawaiian, it skirted the island
Like an ancient fretted lute, brought rhythmic tinkling to Thailand
It danced the Spanish Flamenco in Seville
And, over the Pond, it played country in Nashville

Being showcased on Sixth Street, in Austin, came as a shock
So it surged round the block playing hard rock
When the tour was over it could climb back in its case
The vibrant guitar would vanish without trace.

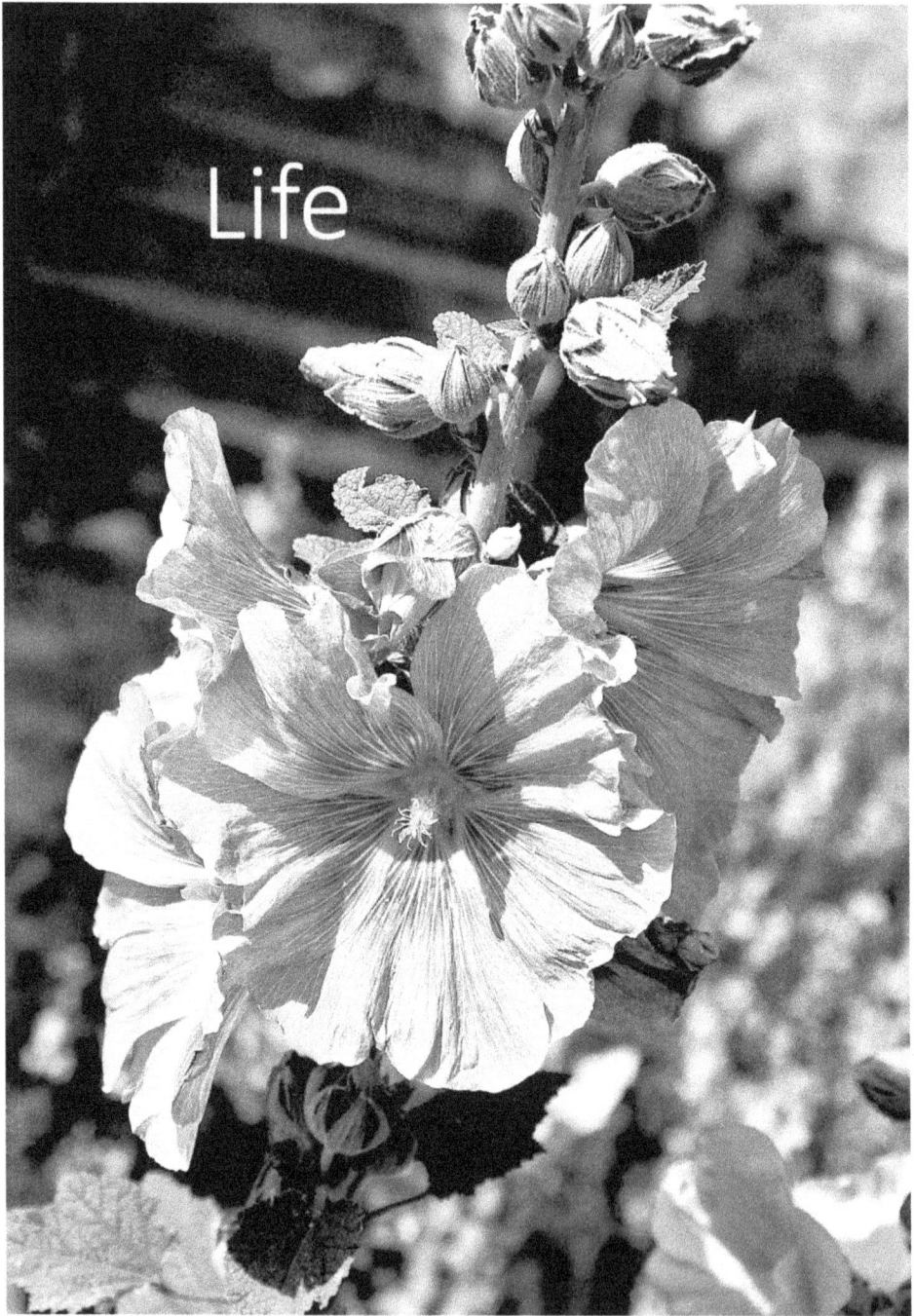

Life

Beckoning [48] - Life

Life's Journey

Flowing lines; intermittent peaks
Undulations; infrequent depths no one seeks
Spontaneous occasions; remote visions
Lots to deal with, to avoid cultural collisions

Control of one's own life, minimizing strife
Much better than trying to catch a falling knife
The hunt is on, be it as a search or pursuit
If you don't give it some shape, its worth can be moot

Like an impressionist, dabbing paint
Each small amount adds to the whole, rather than taint
The thrill of the chase, like travelling to arrive
May often trump the goal for which one might strive

Is there a secret to education, to work, to love or to being?
Do they each have a value, so worth the seeing
No need to be stuck with a quest for perfection or chasing one's tail
The significance of bouncing back and moving on, rather than fail

Seeking answers and inspiration; wondering about each new craze
Driving each of us in various ways
The importance of dreams as we gaze on a maze
We're all on a journey to the end of our days.

Aspects of Life

With a solitary one of anything, how do you maximize its benefit?
It doesn't seem sensible purely to let it degenerate
How to apply it, to the best way to approach your one and only life
Knowing it tends to start and end with relying on others being rife?

Without a strong foundation, how does one find a meaningful anchor?
Is it like a sin of omission which can only lead to rancor?
The value of family should be learnt naturally, without any ambiguity
From loving parents, making us feel we belong; with no hint of insecurity

Where does responsibility lie, as we each grow and take on the world?
We have to learn to take the strain but not by being into a void, hurled
It's not necessarily something to be taken too seriously and get one down
Neither is it the opposite - always being a game and acting the clown

Some may be forced to learn to become streetwise, at an early age
Equally, others shielded and developing alternative skills with which to engage
Along the path, a sense of values, good or bad, imbue each personality
Each discovering facets of one's own sense of reality

Individuality, sexuality, morality, spirituality; but a priority is vitality
The essentials, of aiming for health and energy, driving your actuality
With this in place who knows what you can achieve
The main thing is to find confidence in yourself and to believe

What sort of focus will you have as the years pass?
Do doubt it will change but what might it encompass
Your own family, career and some sort of financial wellbeing
Romance likely features; but consider your latter years - be farseeing

Have you already contributed to communities to which you've belonged
Did you learn forgiveness, of those, by whom you have been wronged
What's your boredom threshold and can you keep yourself entertained
Do you participate or prefer to spectate, as though preordained?

We learn from others, but we need to evaluate and make our own decisions
Challenges, changes and opportunities are things requiring provisions
Accentuating the positive, curtailing the negative and minimizing strife
Being open to new friendships, to adventure and to the spice of life.

Life's Obligation

There is no turning back and you can't stop in your track
Through the jungle of life your way you must hack
Just as no one can stop the march of time
There is no certain route and you won't always be in your prime

However you approach it, you will precede from day to day
Some will be sad, although many may be gay
All have to be lived, in spite of what one might think or say
And no matter how sunny, no matter how gray

At times it can be like climbing a ladder; being forced to go on
Multiple destinations; some might be and some might have gone
No matter what your preference in rollercoaster rides
This is a continuum, from which no one hides

What is it, about a hike on a mountain trail?
Regardless of being strong or despite being frail
It may have some planning; but the influence of our heart
Can produce one, with the whole, greater than the sum of the parts

What more could one ask or how could it be bettered
If we could all, of life's temptations and sins, be unfettered?
It may be going too far and is unlikely to ever be the case
But, we could still play our part, in leaving the world a better place.

Could It Be Yours?

In your wildest dreams
As you perhaps contemplated some of life's themes
A time before and a time to come
Yours may not be the same as mine, with the beat of different drum
How to find, if you are of a mind,
An appreciation of a special kind?

Major, minor, sharp or flat
Something being so in tune with that
That - what is it which wears the cap?

The unthinkingly obvious makes our words or feelings flow with ease
Yet there are times when we cannot see the wood for the trees
Maybe blinkers restrain
Only enable a regular refrain
An unseen lock causing no pain
But its key could release many a subtle gain

A sense of time, a sense of place
When, to display your emotions is no disgrace
Then, at other times and in another sense
Without any effort at pretence
Something triggers in the immediate tense

The sight of a flowering prickly pear
A light aroma in the air
A faint sound of wildlife, maybe, somewhere
A gentle touch, as a moment with someone you share
The hint of a flavor, with which nothing can compare
The value of these five hits home as, at life, you do stare.

Humanity

The whole of humanity or the sum of the humanities
Both containing shades of vanities, insanities and even profanities
Its shifting state is defined by the aggregate of everyone on earth
Physical, mental, emotional and spiritual attributes identify its worth

To move it forward entails love, kindness and social skills
But still leaves room for thrills and paying the bills
Developing understanding, of what is inspiring and meaningful
Can help to avoid the harmful and precipitate the successful

What is it about and why is it important - it's not as though it's a constant?
Participating in change is not to be feared or about which to be reluctant
Where it's been and where it's going have relevance to everyone
You can't live without being part of it, so contribute, before you're gone.

The Best Things in Life are Free

Looking out, the lightning flashed and the thunder crashed
Elsewhere, gentle waves onto a beach splashed
Over a sudden drop, water could not resist the fall
Sighting nature's young will never pall

The smell in the desert of the season's first rain
Something able to reduce potential pain
The scent of an aromatic flower
Gifted with a special power

A rewarding view from a lofty peak
Material, for a nest, in a bird's beak
The combination of a canyon and communion
Rewarding each experience of nature and human union.

Education

Why does education or learning have such an appeal?
Even though being streetwise, for some, may be the alternative deal
Anyway, what does it mean to be educated and why is it so highly rated?
Knowledge, understanding and empathy must be features correlated

Telling the difference between right and wrong, fact and fiction
Not to mention predisposition, misinformation or alternative depiction
Ability to communicate and valuing other points of view are essential
Along the road to appreciating and fulfilling one's potential

Let's not forget the development of character and moral courage
Swift, determined and constructive thinking one should not disparage
Being taught facts is all very well but there are other intangible elements
Concentration, adaptability, creativity, a passion - each compliments

So, as you've developed and become a meaningful part of society
Bear in mind your experiences contributed instructive variety
The process should never stop, as you take risks and defeat impediments
Live life - with integrity and intellectual humility as powerful compliments.

Youth

Different definitions, around the world, but generally 15-24 is the range
It's a special time of appearance, novelty, vitality and rapid change
A period of being - full of experiences, discovery and learning
Not only life and the world, but knowledge about one's self discerning

Excitement and fun yet, at the same time, fears and possible insecurity
Thoughts of the ability to love and be loved, along the road to maturity
Questions of family stability, of education and the need to earn a living
Peer pressure, morals, dangers in various guises - all sources of misgiving

It's so important, as in earlier years, to have support and guidance
When self-confidence runs high it may generate rhetoric with stridence
Fearlessness and invincibility are qualities each having a place
Stepping back from them, at times, should not be thought a disgrace

Building the foundations of one's future is at the heart of the subject
It's full of questions and searching for answers - an important project
It's essential as a balance, alongside the idealism of youth
As one makes one's journey in pursuit of meaning and truth

As you learn to more easily recover from the falls along the way
Physical and emotional confidence grows; self-worth is a bigger play
Developing relationships, appraising values, discovering a comfort zone
All provide nourishment for the seeds of success you will have sown.

Change

Manifestations, regularly seen in the sky, on high
Breaking waves, one tries to ride, with the incoming tide
Rain and drought, what variety of notion do they sprout
Seasons' expressions, the landscape freshens

Fashions follow a similar track, although retro can come back
Popularity reigns, until, for something else, it wanes
Prices, for good or ill, never, for long, standing still
Technology, with self-feeding loops, likes jumping through hoops

Predictability is a useful thing, but the unexpected can often be king
Phenomena happening to advance, driven by chance or even finance
But let's not pretend, we could merely be following a trend
Time and timing - plainly different, or a twist inherent?

Significant transitions, which we realize will be more than suspicions
In the vein of progressing from learning, to the necessity for earning
This part of being is something about which we should be all-seeing
The least appropriate strategy is, from change, ourselves to estrange.

Perceptions

Environment and upbringing have their effect upon the world
Inside of which a multitude of attitudes are curled
Like dimensions, beyond the basic four
Baggage influencing all of us; and to our very core

Countless variations of qualities; weak and strong
You might not like it but to which tribe do you belong
Shows of favoritism, prejudice and of reaching unjustified conclusions
There may be limited collusions but they certainly create illusions

Are these conditions which should be allowed to persist?
How many of us stand up and determine to resist?
To take a balanced view can be difficult to do
Like treating me as fairly as I might like to treat you.

Risk Reward Ratio

To balance the risk against the reward
To make the choice and avoid discord
The potential loss; the likely gain
Which decision will keep you sane?

Will there be second chances
Is there time to find specific answers?
The need to calculate; the urge to gamble
Clear your thoughts - go for a ramble

Joy from exposing one's self to vulnerability
Of opening one's heart to another, with humility
Testing one's ability to survive, even thrive
Going against the flow with determination and drive

What are the consequences of getting it wrong
Is the outcome something for which you long
Aspects of finance or a challenge to emotion
Resolute action or a hesitant notion?

Going It Alone

Why would someone go it alone?
Nowhere to hide and the chance of injured pride.
But then, why would anyone from every risk try to hide?
Surely the alternatives are not something for which to atone
There must be benefits from standing on one's own

An idea, an invention, a concept - which will not go away
The grass is not always greener on the other side
So, are you good at taking challenges in your stride?
Disappointment, frustration, envy - could they have a say
In this new game you're about to play?

There's a sense of identity derived from individuality
It's very distinct from being a valued member of a group
The psychology has one jumping through a very different hoop
Some can be both - a Jekyll and Hyde duality
Leading a life filled with variety and vitality.

Difficulty in Letting Go

Sounds, images, experiences - memories flashing across one's mind
Feelings you don't wish to be without, as though stars are still aligned
Equally, it may be fear of the unknown or doing something on one's own
Then, again, it may be breaking a habit, one needing to be overthrown

Life is all about hope and, at times, it can capture us, like a rope
How does one know when to abandon it and find another way to cope?
Such are decisions in life - how to carry on and curtail mental collisions
Trying to maximize quality - avoiding inadvisable divisions

How to tackle this to good effect, even though the result may be imperfect?
No prevarication, but acting until deeds produce the best aftereffect
The positive impact, of not standing still, will bring you in from the cold
Now, with partitioned memories and new hope having taken hold.

Burning Bridges and Crossing Thresholds

The bridge collapsed, as its wooden structure was consumed by fire
Had I made the right choice, before things became so dire
I'd slammed the door behind me and, now, it would be forever locked
Future channels of possible escape I'd foolishly blocked

The nightmare continued, as I tossed and turned in bed
My actions were going against everything I'd ever read
Had I acted out of impatience and sheer bottled-up frustration
And, now, I was on my way, in haste, to a body language demonstration

How long would this go on and would I have regrets
Was it wise to be negative when the other party never forgets?
Saved, I awoke, the sun came shining in
Thresholds, Rubicons, new thought processes could begin.

Love

Manifestations, with a diversity of forms, sought or experienced in life
Unfortunately, not always for one's fellow human being; or without strife
However, let's concentrate on advantages - to the individual and to society
Strengths, instead of activities which lead to impropriety, even notoriety

As it develops, at its strongest, it becomes unconditional
And, for religions around the world, to preach about it is traditional
The essence of a strong family, influencing blood being thicker than water
If the members were bricks, it would be their binding mortar

Such is not to say it can't be strong towards others, activities and stuff
It's especially useful in times of difficulty when the going gets tough
In a milder form, treating others as you would like to be treated
Is a wonderful approach to practice and be regularly repeated

There is an interesting dichotomy, as to what is love and what is passion
Intenseness of deep affection versus strong and tricky to control emotion
Loving someone, warts and all, as opposed to making love
Which definition do you prefer - when push comes to shove?

Eternal Triangle

Have you ever thought of standing a triangle on its edge?
You could even try balancing it on a ledge
How would it work and what could go wrong
Which of the three might need to prove strong?

Could its shape change from isosceles to equilateral
And what if a certain two took decisions unilateral
Would the third have drawn the short straw
But, nevertheless, still return, asking for more?

If two equal sides were compressed into one
There would be no need for the third, it would have been and gone
What if it sprang back and forced the other two apart
Could it relate to an affair of the heart?

An unlikely supposition, leading to a change of position
The dream of an earlier decision, open to revision
Fairytales and figments of the imagination
Seeking a new relationship and a route to its creation

Limited combinations of one, two or three
Despite certain wishes, which one might it be?
A matched pair and one curled into a circle infernal
For ever interlocked, with a degree of pain eternal?

Losing Love

What is it about love which attracts the word unconditional?
Might one consider it a bold idea - traditional?
What is the difference between when one gives and when one receives?
Especially if the receiver changes and deceives

It suggests it was not a two-way street, but still one gives and hopes
Does this take you down nothing but a series of slippery slopes?
A love which may never die, no matter how hard you might try
It breaks your heart and it makes you cry

There have been wonderful times and promises of marriage
Which, somehow, the other, very much, came to disparage
The disappointment of losing what should have been
Made worse, when, with another person seen

One can lose control of one's mind
Almost like an obsession one did find
Feeling so low; and in the depths of despair
There seemed no way one's mind to repair

Such a distraction from other aspects of life
How could one start to reduce this form of strife?
Which was more important - to hate or forgive?
Forgiveness is healing and hating - destructive

Opening one's heart, even to a friend, may make one feel more vulnerable
But, if it is right, it is like a gift - wonderful
It could bring tears which may rescue your fears
But your situation needs a new kind of hope for future years

Many things are easier said than done
But there are times in life when the battle must be won
The time when a friend in need is a friend indeed
The moment one's heart finds a way to start to stop the need to bleed

Letting it go and letting it show
Maybe giving your heart something of a new glow
One could have found something to replace a little of what one has lost
And the threshold, to the start of recovery, finally crossed.

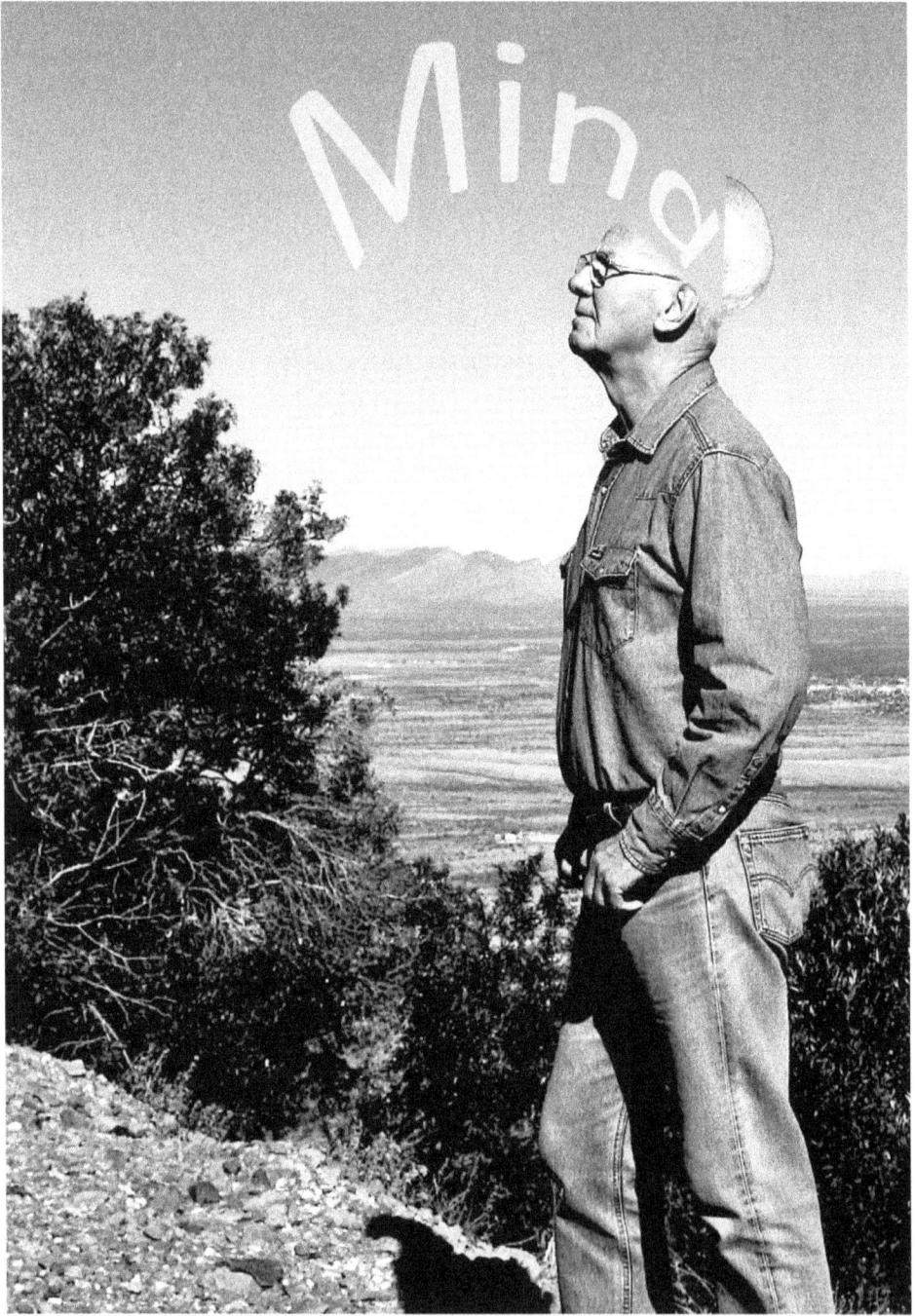

Beckoning [68] - Mind

In sleep

Air, space, ethereal matter
Colors, shapes in kaleidoscopic patterns
Darkness, light make random movements and time
The relative source of life's great moments
Through it all allows no recapture
Not for them who would escape it nor,
Although some would protest its unreality,
Can such things defy any degree of rationality.

In many ways, past or future, there is a closeness
An inescapable aura of what could or might have been
And then, when seeming actuality, something of great power
Its intenseness no longer imagined
Causes physical action, with a suddenness which may not be denied

It ends as with a start, as some would say, intense of feeling
Passion, fear, the unexpected climax about to unfold
The dawn to break or perhaps, more likely past
A shake of the head, a stirring of the limbs
The comfort of a partner's warmth or the emptiness of being alone
It is over, it was not real.

Memories

Evocative or provocative are words which play with the mind
Sometimes unkind but, more often, positive we find
The nature of being and trying to be all-seeing
It leaves us with impressions
Good or, at times, bad
Maybe some we even wish we'd never had
But, still, we can recall our favorite ones of all
The ones which never pall
And some, maybe, where we tumbled or took a fall
But, usually, the ones expressing the best
Come back into our minds without any behest.

Body and Mind

One hears idle chatter about mind over matter
So, let's sit down and see if we can have our own stimulating natter
The mind is contained within the body, from which there is no escape
Yes, but not an unchanging relationship, with rules and red tape

Nevertheless, is there any way to make predictions
Or are we faced with endless contradictions?
It could be, but I don't think we'd dispute some correlation
And there's no way either can act in isolation

The mind drives ambition which, in turn, can drive the body
What does it tell us about the liaison we each embody?
Pain may be a manifestation of the body, manipulated by the mind
Hang on, if mind is part of the brain, our discussion could become a bind

Let's move on and consider a few typical perceptions
Appearances can be deceptive, even though there are many exceptions
A short step to one's own view of one's self image
What one see's is what one gets? Assuming so may result in damage

But our minds can play tricks on us and we don't always feel in control
Be careful, you'll soon be telling me we're influenced by the soul
Well, it's not exactly simple; as I can see you appreciate
So, perhaps we'd better leave further discussion until our next blind date

Before we go, there is something to which I'd like to make an allusion
I can cope with it, so long as it's not an illusion
Perhaps worthy of thought before we meet again, hence the mention
Body, brain, mind, soul - sources of positive energy or adverse tension?

Aspects of Self

Self-actualization - is it really understood?
Are some interpretations like being blinkered and wearing a hood?
They suggest selfishness becomes a leading characteristic
For me it's misleading and most certainly not realistic

No doubt it exists, to some degree
It's not unlike giving to receive, you see
But what does it take to be truly fulfilled
What related thoughts, through the mind, might be milled?

Knowing one's self would make a wonderful start
Without it, how could one be sure of putting the horse before the cart?
An easy step from there to knowing how, to one's self to be true
Being comfortable in one's own skin - your confidence would renew

If you know who and what you are, do you know what you'd like to be?
To succeed would entail self discipline and control, I suspect you'd agree
A degree of independence to achieve self-discovery may be essential
And a measure of enlightened self-interest could help fulfill your potential

Somehow there's a lack of balance on the scales
Except I can't imagine you're as hard as nails
There must be some virtue and selflessness; and a lack of being conceited
In anyone who treats others as they, themselves, would like to be treated

So, don't be a prisoner of your own mind or of a selfish mentality
Laugh at yourself, as you develop your own personality
Never forget this life and our world is all about cooperation
Existing in isolation is impossible and could only lead to desperation.

Philosophy

Sat on the patio, July 2015, Venus, with Jupiter nearby, could be seen
It inspired me in ways philosophical. I felt relaxed and serene
My mind came alive, inspiring a creative drive
I had no hesitation, as into this subject I did dive

Thoughts, complimented by a shot of tequila and tree frogs in song
Are you a philosopher or philosophical and strong?
In so many ways it's easier to accept perceived wisdom
But it's wonderful to think outside the box and experience its freedom

There are so many questions to ask and answers to seek
Considering existence, knowledge and reality is not for the meek
It stimulates and challenges one's conceptual abilities
And one's views may make one open to possible hostilities

With any form of critical thinking, there are times not for blinking
The alternative meaning indicates, from calmness, no shrinking
Its main purpose - to universally elucidate aspects unsolved by science
Truth, significance and wisdom - lacking techniques for total compliance.

Search for Perfection

Define, measure, rate
Improve, enhance, create
A new record, a better score; always scope for a little more
Never satisfied, the quality going to the core

What is it about - connections with the moon?
The imperative achievement - despite no way, soon
Money, fame, personal satisfaction or some other driver
What is the essence of the ultimate striver?

The route may be different, for an art or a science
But always, of failure, standing in defiance
Consider what makes for perfection in any setting
You may achieve it by chance, but I wouldn't be betting.

Work

To be successful requires conscientiousness and giving of one's best
It pays to act smart, but it's not the only feature in which to invest
No doubt luck, and being in the right place at the right time,
Also contribute to crafting a worthwhile and progressive climb

No one wants to be on a downhill and deteriorating slope
But, with this ethic, comes moral benefit, not purely relying on hope
A strengthened character results from tenacity, diligence and willpower
If they haven't already, positive qualities, from this, will flower

Whether working alone or as part of a team, discipline and responsibility
Come together to progress towards excellence and enhanced capability
If you stand up to be counted, will others enable a defense to be mounted
Will integrity and all the other important attributes, for you, be accounted?

Leaders and Followers

To do or to spectate, with which would you prefer a date
And, what about leading a race, but only as the person setting the pace?
How much do you care, if you're in a huge crowd, in a square
Or attending a political rally, in a mammoth stadium, in a deep valley?

In a smaller setting, how would we open the betting?
Go for role reversal, or worry about the need for serious rehearsal
Do you have strong points of view, or prefer to take someone else's cue
When everyone else is in a panic, are you calm or somewhat frantic?

Having asked so many questions, it's fair to make a few suggestions
Talking suggestions, many people prefer answers to questions
Most important - fine leaders need first-rate followers, not just heeders
At the extremes, dictators and alienators are inferior, weakening teams

We all have comfort zones; about which the majority would make no bones
Yet most would like to progress in some way, not just sit around and play
Between extreme ambition and no iota, what is the mix to fill your quota?
It's like both sides of the middle - sometimes lead or be second fiddle.

Pride

What is it about and why is it felt
Hardly much relevance in how the cards were dealt
A swelling heart or a figure standing tall
Are these the rewards of answering the call?

If you've never experienced it you probably haven't tried
Maybe you've been fooling and, even to yourself, lied
For some it may come from the results of others
Rewarding supportive fathers and those very caring mothers

Family and friends is not where it ends
And it's never too late to make some sort of amends
For example, in the workplace and whatever one's role
It shouldn't be necessary for others, you to cajole

However small, however big
This is a jewel for which you should dig
Like most things worthwhile, it doesn't grow on trees
Nor will it be found blowing in the breeze

So seek something on which to focus
Don't aim to delegate to a stand-in locus
Even if you need help, stand on your own two feet
Then it shouldn't be too long before this quality you greet

Oh, and one more thing, before you get too relaxed
Don't forget there are times when it should never be completely axed
With the boot on the other foot, don't leave others with nowhere to hide
However negative, they also need leaving with at least some pride.

Superiority and Inferiority Complexes

Of all the states of mind, two may be considered a bind
The perspective changes, depending on which, in someone else, you find
If you're honest, you may have discovered something about yourself
As I once did and was able to change - about myself

Neither would be considered a desirable trait
Both would be better never let out of the starting gate
Having taken root, each can grow - like a weed
To the point, where serious control is what they need

Looking down from above will not inspire love
But rising up from underneath demands an inspiring shove
If you possess one or the other; and to pay attention is your desire,
Find some kindling and ignite the self-improvement fire.

Competition

Does it speak to your mind, your body or fall on deaf ears
Maybe it's something activating your greatest fears
How do you fare amongst your peers
When you are in the midst of it, do you fall into arrears?

What can be done to narrow the gap and make sure you don't snap?
The last thing you need is to feel you've got caught in a trap
So, let's consider angles, both physical and mental
We need to get you on an upwards trajectory, with gains incremental

It's all very well having strength, stamina, being supple and healthy
But those, alone, won't take you far on the road to being a touch wealthy
Many things affect the outcome, as an individual or a member of a team
What we need to do is come up with a plan or some sort of scheme

It's better to have empathy, understanding, respect and consideration
These facets could provide some essential acceleration
The last thing you need is cynicism, rage or hostility
Much better to be focused, find the will to win and accept responsibility

Let's finish by outlining attributes which could help, as you advance -
Having a sense of purpose, self-esteem and confidence would enhance
Being practical and dealing with change would improve your chance
Interpersonal skills and confidence, aiding an improved competitive stance.

Eating the Elephant

A different texture, a different taste
Whatever else, don't let your efforts go to waste
From the head to the tail or the tail to the head
Either way, don't stop yourself, get up and out of bed

Now, break it down into an ear or the tail
Thinking of even a leg, too soon, could set you up to fail
My mother used to talk about 'a little and often'
It sure helped me - many a target to soften

Small bites or big bites, small decisions or big decisions
Small bites, small decisions, train the molars for larger incisions
Having sharpened your teeth, you are more ready to succeed
Gaining lots of satisfaction with each mouthful - satiating the greed.

Passion and Enthusiasm

Enthusiasm morphed into passion, becoming a dual reinforcing mechanism
Passion entailing enthusiasm, but the opposite may be a form of illusionism
Two major factors in life - some, carried away with; others can't find at all
Do they both start from specific interest - putting drive and energy on call?

We all vary as to which subjects turn us on and which leave us cold
But time is of the essence - have it, find it, make it or put follow-up on hold
There are those, whose desires, they have no means of achieving
Rather like the frustration of having a dream for which you are grieving

Do you ever reflect on how fortunate you must be and express gratitude
Or do you take such things for granted and display a non-caring attitude?
Never stop; but don't get carried away with it in a detrimental fashion
Spare a thought for others, as you enthusiastically chase your passion.

From Whence Willpower?

On the edge of a canyon with nowhere to hide
Stood discipline and willpower, conversing with pride
Do you remember when you were living out of control?
I certainly do and I thought it had damaged my soul

It resonates worth me, as I'm sure we'd both agree
But, once in a while, the benefits we confer are difficult to see
That's very true although, sometimes, we can be found out of the blue
It could be when a greater power suddenly comes into view

Yes, but it may also be when one sees the light
Like flicking a switch in the dark of the night
There are alternatives - for me it was much more gradual
What, a bit like sparring in the throes of a dual?

Correct, which contender would win was so difficult to detect
I was a suspect with a future to protect
Finding the strength I needed was so up and down
But, eventually, I got there and now wear a crown, instead of a frown

Maybe we both need a sense of direction
Could be; it may offer a form of protection
Like the fence against which we now lean
Just look at that drop - it's horribly mean!

The Nature of Attention

Attention   Attention   **Attention - Please!**

A sign   A focus   A passion
Whatever form, it can be demanding
Like a baby, effectively commanding

And then,   and then   and then again
There may be a particular hidden or apparent need
A leader, an invalid, a performing star
The call may be from near or far
It may need a reaction or be best ignored
Perhaps a fire or other calamity
Or a seeker who makes you bored
It leads to decisions and forms of judgment
Time for patience or response most urgent

Subtle   obvious   **or even screaming!**

Communications

There are shades of ability when it comes to relating to others
Could they have been influenced by our fathers and our mothers?
From crying, as a baby, all the way to one's own eulogy
Encompassing electronics and manifestations of biology

Whatever form they take, there's always sender, receiver and message
The trick is to use the right words, ensuring a meaningful passage
Even then, both parties would benefit from understanding the context
Unless one is scheming and plotting, no reason for an illusory pretext

Needless to say, there are all sorts of potential complications
Tenor of voice, body language and even clothes can cause evocations
People, face to face, are so much better than being in different locations
It means there is every chance of noticing direct or implicit indications

Observing emotions, ideas, opinions or thoughts - one can accept or refuse
Not to mention the impact of aftershave, perfumes, piercings, BO or tattoos
But spare a thought for those who are deaf or blind
How do they fare and, to them, is it easier to be unkind?

Physical and mental impairment are not the best things for empowerment
Yet, without effective interactions, how to aspire to betterment?
For everyone there are also characteristics of culture and gender
But the last thing one wants to do is, to failure, surrender

Electronics and surveillance demand responses and careful confidentiality
An added question of how do we interpret all the forms of virtual reality?
The striking attribute, appearing at times to be in danger of disappearing
Is to make sure we have aptitude for true listening and not simply hearing.

Ethics and Choices

Honest, serene, effortlessly flowing
How can it be, when you know what you're knowing
Are you putting on a front
Have you got any sort of conscience in the hunt?

Have you considered your good fortune in being able to make choices
Or do you find it a problem, like being talked at by too many voices?
Perhaps it's rather like learning any difficult art
It needs regular practice - a strong skill set to impart

Of course, I could be doing you a disservice and I may be misguided
So, let's change course - further worthwhile thoughts to be provided
We understand moral principles and concepts of right and wrong
But, at times, it can be very difficult to decide in which camp we belong

There are occasions when there is no escape and we are forced to choose
Fairness or decisions for the good of society we cannot lightly refuse
Rules of conduct, of which to be proud, should be sought lifelong
When choice is no choice, because your ethical values are strong.

Optimism and Pessimism

Some may consider talk, of how full is the glass, as being rather crass
So, I hope you won't think, the following words, are full of gas
They almost come from opposite ends of the spectrum
And reputedly didn't come out of anyone's rectum!

Let's start with any situation with a focal point
Could it lead to success or purely disappoint
And what if the objective is to avoid a negative
Would it turn the tables, however tentative?

This isn't the time to prevaricate or even to rationalize
But, it may be appropriate, one's thoughts, to analyze
Across the divide, of half empty or half full
The thought of a preference you might like to mull

Now, how much of a difference do you think it might make
Having decided which approach you're going to take?
Is this the way you've always tended to think before
Or are you getting bored and tending to want to snore?

Are our views the results of decisions
Do we display consistency or vary with our positions?
Some, by nature, may be more one way than the other
And you'd hardly class the opposite as being like a brother

So, where do you stand and are you stuck in a mold
Like the pessimist who can sometimes get left out in the cold
Or do you see the bright side and remain full of hope
Finding life, as an optimist, a much better way to cope?

Adventure

Define it, plan it, do it!
Forget that, risk it - head for the unknown
That's all very well; but what the hell
Calculated risks strike my bell

Oh come on - do something on the fly
Not meaning to pry, but is there a reason why?
Maybe; to share an aspect
Aging trends affect the intellect; what to reject

Sounds of conservatism alarm
What happened - the door, the barn?
Let it escape, it's not too late
Climb the mountain, elevate the mind

True, it's all downhill from there
Opportune to abandon care
Let the wind blow through the hair
Perhaps seeking is the way to find?

Curiosity, Knowledge and Understanding

Do you remember that cat; well it's still alive, despite its curiosity
Sometimes it purrs, as though understanding its owner's generosity
On a different occasion it got stuck up a tree and had to be retrieved
Its knowledge of climbing, sadly, from consequences deceived

It sounds like questions and answers and meaningful interpretations
Quality of information leading to irritations or vital adaptations
Some say you can't have understanding unless you have knowledge first
On such a basis, what could be better than an unquenchable thirst?

Maybe to be inquisitive or have a good memory is a prerequisite
On the road to developing a capacity for comprehension exquisite
In essence, surely none of this will be to any avail
Unless benefits to the present or future are seen to prevail?

Empathy, Sympathy and Understanding

Those look like a difficult pair of shoes to wear
You could try them and see if you still care
Would you like to know how they came to be in such a condition?
If I did, it might influence my position

When did you last walk in someone else's shoes?
You may have found it offered some unexpected clues
Indeed, you are right. The first time I tried it gave me a fright
But it certainly changed my view, when I suddenly saw the light

I wonder what prompted you to take such an approach?
It didn't come naturally and, now, myself I reproach
Did you feel your relationships weren't all they might have been?
It was as though my perspective was all I'd ever seen

Maybe it was the time when you started to appreciate critical thinking?
It surely resonates as something from which one should not be shrinking
The interesting thing was when I tried to imagine alternative possibilities
It suddenly gave me awareness of how to improve my people abilities

There are lots of individuals who are still like you used to be
Yes, I can see it now but, originally, you'd never have got me to agree
I suspect it's like any form of understanding
The horizons and quality of life, contributing to continuously expanding.

Humility

From the top of a mountain, with a clarion call
Confidence, infallibility - a great height from which to fall
To lose a friend; to drive others round the bend
With their patience, on occasion, leading them to pretend

The competitive spirit, the touch of inferiority
Hidden on occasion by a display of superiority
What does it take to appreciate the lot of others
To leave a little pride and become like brothers?

Never Missing What You've Never Had

Should there ever be any concern for the unknown?
Define unknown aware and unknown unknown
What an extraordinary request; but it is at your behest
Do your best to pass the test
Yes, without an answer can one ever rest?

No questions - no answers needed
Those who have, and lose, find a problem seeded
Those without, who still don't know, should have their bliss heeded
But is it really so simple
It's not exactly like discovering a pimple?

Who said "Curiosity killed the cat"?
Temptation - we all know who were good at that
Quantification of benefit and risk - in advance
Which may do so much, the imagination to enhance
Can often lead to playing the laws of chance.

Patience and Having a Sense of Purpose

The hands turn; the digits change sequentially
Stomachs churn; action, results, change - potentially
A game of cards; the climbing of a mountain
Broken shards; reconstruction of a fountain

Developing a theme; fulfilling a dream
Understanding a scheme; building a team
Difficult negotiations; certain amazing creations
Building nations; avoiding temptations

The passage of time, unlike unsullied white light
Ebbing and flowing until the objective comes into sight
Beating huge challenges produces enormous fulfillment
What is needed is the key to evolutionary improvement.

Conceptual and Critical Thinking

Do you have any concept of what it means to be critically thinking
Or would you rather be with your friends, in a bar, drinking?
Now, there's a thought, but it might be somewhat egocentric
Besides, we'd probably finish up with conversation concentric

You can go and join them if you wish, I wouldn't think of you as selfish
All thoughts of cognitive processes and self-discipline you could banish
No, no, let's explore this further; act as though intellect is in season
Besides, it may surprise you, but I'm fascinated by abstraction and reason

Hang on, you'll get in front of me and there'll be nothing to debate
We're seeking connections, not aspects to ignore or mediocre to exacerbate
Well, I know much thinking is distorted, uninformed or narrow-minded
If we're to improve the quality of life, to this subject we can't be blinded

You could be right; and I'm glad you haven't taken fright
Having stimulating discussion is such a delight
Yes, it's good to get away from the obvious and consider alternatives
We'll never get anywhere if we become bogged down in palliatives

I've decided you have knowledge of concepts and skill in thinking
And there's no sign of your, from insightful levels of thought, shrinking
I try to be fair and consider implications; and other points of view
It takes intellectual humility, but I hope the results come shining through.

Confidence, Trust and Secrets

Positive emotions, we shower on others, entail guarding against gullibility
However, very special, if on someone known for their dependability
No one is infallible, but it's so comforting to confer without hesitation
To live in any other way can give rise to constraints or exasperation

How do you build confidence or trust; and why secrets
Are either of the former two way streets; the latter, hiding regrets?
These questions run deep, especially for matters of state
They're all interlinked; being inputs influencing fate

Suspicion of being compromised can cause anxiety; even fear
Shades of vulnerability add another layer; another frontier
We could play with words - having it or sharing one - confidence
They both seem relevant to the discussion - coincidence?

We're talking of considerations with the ability to unite or divide
Their power, in this sense, should be appreciated, not decried
Do you trust in anyone, sufficiently, a secret to confidently share?
Maybe, sometimes, it could be to a stranger your inner self you declare.

Temptation

To accept or reject - such is the key
Like a fact of life for all to see
Is it so obvious; a siren sounding the alarm
Warning of the possibility of insidious harm
A fancy, a liking, a need - a demand
Search, find - decide who is in command
Under what guise will it present itself today?
Challenging the seeker to find in the hay
Then, when the discovery is made
Is the time resolve will start to fade
How to avoid the slippery slope
Without seeking help from an Imam or the Pope?
The game may be short or it may be long
Willpower and self-control - the essentials of being strong.

Subconscious

What is it? Do we ever really know it?
Is it related to conscience or are scruples no sort of fit
What are the influences which bring it into play
Can we ever quantify the ways in which it has a say?

A sudden involuntary action; a thought out of the blue
From whence do these things get their unexplained cue?
The deep well, within the mind, hiding submerged codes
Not the same, but reminiscent of signs at the sides of roads

Electronic impulses; sudden flashes of lightning
At once enlightening; sometimes downright frightening
A sign of confirmation, a prompt for inspiration
Occasionally, an immediate and surprising transformation

A lifetime of exposure, of learning, of experience
Creates a shadow being, influencing strictness or lenience
At the other extreme, words in conversation may flow
Dealing the unexpecting recipient an insulting blow

Out of character or of real self, glimpses of exposure?
To this question, endless analysis will never bring closure
One's internal value system is not easy to change
So, when it takes you over, it can be rather strange.

Road to Forgiveness

Why it happened is hard to explain
Causing degrees of pain - again and again
From the flesh to the mind, creating a real bind
Was this the way to go on or could it be left behind?

The past was the past and it could not be changed
Such mixed up notions crying to be rearranged
Was there a way to move on from this state?
The last thing to do was to live on and spread hate

The energy spent on these thoughts could be put to better use
Things so much more positive than spreading abuse
Maybe one could aim to direct to forget
True peace of mind to try and beget

But ill-discipline may let feelings come rushing back
Stopping one's progress dead in its track
Maybe forgetting hints of a form of selfishness
When the true route to healing calls for forgiveness?

Relaxation

All of a sudden, I started to yawn
The fact my stress had lifted, started to dawn
Was there a lesson I should countenance
The balance between submission and dominance?
In the extreme was it like a cat without cream
Maybe switch off and find time to daydream
It appears under different guises
Some known faces; but others, unexpected surprises
The company of good friends or receiving gratitude
An unanticipated smile or a space for solitude
Repeated breaking of waves on a shoreline
Observing stars on a clear night, high above the skyline
The arts, nature, sport - exercises, physical and mental
Activities without pressure and so little detrimental.

Emotions

Do you know how many affective states of consciousness are presented
More importantly, by which is your mind most commonly frequented?
What are the influences bringing them into play, does empathy have a say?
More likely, instinctive reactions to earlier value judgments are on display

For every one which is positive, a negative equivalent is not far away
You know the ones I mean; those you hope won't, their welcome, outstay
Regrettably, both good and bad, on occasion, may surface out of control
Even, at times, so extreme, some need help to dig themselves out of a hole

Many seek highs - chasing excitement or forms of happiness and pleasure
Others overtaken by loneliness, sorrow or despair; all are hard to measure
Whilst they may be considered components of a game of hide and seek
Manipulating your own can be beyond technique and filled with mystique

They are not only in one's mind or figments of one's imagination
They have physical symptoms, display control and influence motivation
We need one extreme to appreciate the other; even when not simultaneous
Our genes evolved to help us react to our world, in ways spontaneous.

Impatience and Frustration

Impatient because you're frustrated; or frustrated because you're impatient
It's a conundrum. Which gives which momentum - a question ancient?
Emotions closely linked; and, to be succinct, they're far from extinct
They'll never go away; we must find restraint, not react by pure instinct

In small doses, they can be positive attributes and provide motivation
When they do, they are worthy of careful cultivation
Taking either, beyond a certain point, is very likely to be self-defeating
Any possible, ensuing satisfaction, unlikely to be more than fleeting

Now the waters become gray, depending at whom either is directed
At one's self may be OK; at others - lead to being rejected, not respected
When self-inflicted, might perfectionist tendencies be the cause?
There's a question which may give a person food, their thoughts, to pause

These 'qualities', directed at others, can lead to charges of selfishness
To maintain such a stance leads down the track of foolishness
Impatience for transformation; frustration over failure to achieve or change
As with other negative emotions, there's a call, one's priorities to rearrange

When it comes to youngsters, those who are still learning self-control,
Encouraging them to continue, but try harder, may only dig a deeper hole
The danger, for adults and children, is ceasing to think or act rationally
A priority is to develop the appropriate restraint and mature emotionally.

Insecurity and Feeling Threatened

This is another chicken and egg problem, but let's not put it to the test
Trying to minimize these characteristics can be a perpetual pest
No one goes through life totally free of either or both
Finding a way of dealing with them can be a sign of personal growth

The initial step may seem odd, but it's all about getting to know one's self
We're all individuals, not defined like packages picked off a shelf
It goes beyond such considerations, to feeling secure in one's own skin
This helps to improve confidence; and increase your will to win

These personal traits, real or imagined, may play tricks inside the head
We need to practice and train ourselves not to be filled with fear or dread
One may be insecure, compared to others, or by not sensing much backing
Equally, because of a relationship failure or tragic turn of events attacking

Feeling threatened by a rival's success - causing jealousy or resentment
These are not the things you need on the road to finding contentment
Neither are some of the symptoms, displayed by someone affected
They are things you should work on, from them to ensure you're protected

Consider a few - like being defensive, materialistic or needing attention
What about negative aspects of relationships; all requiring prevention
Awareness of the situation may help towards restoring emotional vigor
No one's perfect, so laughing at one's self can create a beneficial trigger.

Fear

It can strike in an instant or be like insidiousness, developing
From an immediate situation or a speculation wildly galloping
It may be short-lived, relieved by a change in conditions
Or may go on forever, controlled by a phobia with hidden ambitions

This is not the way to live one's life; but it may be easier said than done
Most people value life and don't want to be on a psychological run
There may be a correlation, relating to the degree of risk
To be averse to such things may raise the stakes, in a fashion brisk

One's age at the time can alter one's perception of magnitude
Needless to say, the unknown or uncertain can also affect one's attitude
The desire is to reduce or completely eliminate
How does one find the strength and from whence does it emanate?

In considering it, one has to accept variations from person to person
Most we can deal with but, for no apparent reason, others worsen
There is no single answer or any form of magical pill
But the crux of the matter is to face up to it; and go for the kill.

Stress or Pressure?

If you had to make a choice, P comes before S, it's obvious
Perhaps it's not quite right - leaving you feeling dubious
Of course, you may have other priorities and other decisions to make
Always the pressing deadline, causing you to leave waves in your wake

There may be uncertainty, which you may or may not be able to resolve
If you're in the hands of others, your concern may not dissolve
You could start counting up to ten, as the tension mounts again
Especially if you're hemmed in, with no escape from a virtual pen

A sudden realization - you've turned into a cul-de-sac
Oh grief, opposition forces, their sights trained on your back
Now, let's review our earlier question and see if the fog's cleared
To be able or not to be able to do something - which is more feared?

Familiarity Breeding Contempt

'Ignorance is bliss.' 'A little knowledge is a dangerous thing.'
Two of life's platitudes, which in our ears might ring
Is this a progression where the exception proves the rule?
Perhaps, for limited aspects of understanding, each is a useful verbal tool?

'You can have too much of a good thing' is another to add to the collection
And what if it's an activity for which one has always had a predilection
Does one get tired of one's own body; or the love which forever grows
Not to mention a passion in life, which perpetually flows?

So what might be the exceptions one should take care to appreciate?
Maybe there is a person with whom you no longer associate
Or your favorite food, eaten so often; once more and you'd come unglued
In extreme, reflecting on the concept of heaven, might you be subdued?

The last was a provocative line and, before it, you were doing fine
As a result, our relationship may now be in decline
Perhaps, prior to this, from extreme criticism you had been exempt
It's no longer possible to take anything for granted - nor attempt.

Cynicism

Did you ever come across a cynic, when looking in the mirror
Or meet someone whose negative views couldn't have been clearer?
What about occasional friends, those forever motivated by self-interest
Do you respond to their comments with a measure of disinterest?

Now, someone once said to me 'A cynic is someone who tells the truth'
It made me think and contributed to turning me into something of a sleuth
Maybe I had a propensity in that direction, which only needed a nudge
But, the last thing I'd want to do is any source of learning begrudge

On another occasion, the comment was 'No good deed goes unpunished'
What could it mean; was it like kindness about to be vanquished?
I can't imagine it being a very popular thing to do
If it did happen it could cause a serious hullabaloo

Others say, if you go the cynic's way, you may not be liked or loved
To test the theory, down that road, is not a direction I wish to be shoved
So, at the end of the day, is there anything positive, about it, to say
'Not getting hurt'; and 'Never believing politicians' - unlikely hearsay?

Manipulation, Prevarication, Procrastination and Rationalization

Would you ever consider manipulating things to string people along?
Prevaricating, procrastinating and rationalizing, like nothing was wrong
It sounds more like the work of politicians and religious persuaders
We all do them to some degree - to say otherwise would make us evaders

How does one discern what might be going on, or any hint of a con
The dividing line in accepting or rejecting situations we come upon?
We all have our own standards, as we search for ways to move forwards
Sometimes we may break them, to avoid moving backwards

Everyone is impacted by these traits, even down to the very young
You must have heard them and the manipulative songs they've sung
Are they so different to what's beamed to your TV or electronic device?
When you watch an advert, does the content make you think twice?

Do you set arbitrary deadlines, lie to yourself, defer things until tomorrow
Give yourself rational explanations, after the event, to avoid sorrow?
What is their purpose, are they necessary or excuses of various kinds
About influencing others or one's self and playing games with our minds?

Prejudice and Discrimination

Prejudice leads to discrimination; in turn symptomatic of predisposition
Is either of these activities one about which you would make an admission
Have you ever had these characteristics turned against you?
If not, how often do you try to see the other person's point of view?

Regardless of whether they are fair or not, they highlight diversity
They lead to forms of conflict and, for some, result in adversity
Think of age, ethnicity, gender, health, religion or sexual orientation
There are others and they are all unfortunate reasons for lamentation

Lack of understanding, feeling threatened or some type of insecurity
Lead in this direction and could even be caused by a degree of immaturity
To minimize their impact, to many, is a worthwhile objective
Will you be one to think or act from such a considered perspective?

Hypocrisy

Surely, for someone so true, the word could not apply to you
Could anyone ever live with no double standards to accrue
Is it a matter of degree or knowing it applied to you but not me
Perhaps it has to do with rationalization and setting one's self free?

If there are benefits to minor variations on the theme
At what point is the line crossed; might one deem?
It could be like telling petty lies; to avoid hurting someone's feelings
But perjuring yourself is not the way to enhance your dealings

Like black, white and shades of gray; we discussed those the other day
Regardless of what we say or do, are they all here, to stay
Assuming so, what level of acceptance should we declare
Or should we replicate the sin and proceed as though unaware?

Terrorism

Bullets, bombs, planes - death and destruction, including self-sacrifice
Bio, cyber, eco, narco, nuclear - all approaches which entice
Often using fear to advance objectives - political, religious or secular
Some for financial gain; but everyone aiming for results spectacular

Short-term, one can strive for prevention, rather than addressing causes
It's likely any future respite will turn out to be nothing but pauses
A world, largely governed by pressing priorities, could miss its way
Chasing justice for the guilty, from the best strategy, may lead astray

What would be the essentials, in the quest for an alternative solution?
Understanding the motivation would make an imperative contribution
How extreme would you or I be if placed in a sufficiently acute situation?
Would we never resort to such tactics, especially after careful evaluation?

Polarization

In science, like poles repel; unlike poles attract - facts through and through
But we're concerned with opinions and politics were the reverse is true
With such a connotation, we are talking about views which are poles apart
Deeply held and at opposite ends of the spectrum; but from the heart

They can't both be right and it's possible both may be wrong
Yet, rather than compromise, conflict is likely to come on strong
It may get so bad there's not the slightest attempt to create rapport
At its worst, it results in disrespect and fear, even to the point of war

With groups, there is a tendency to greater extremes - in either direction
As though strength in numbers creates a stronger disconnection
In some ways, it relates to aspects of discrimination
Maybe, compounded by parents leading children into imitation?

There must be a way to reduce its negative impact
It would need many people not to overreact and display much more tact
Overcoming any sense of insecurity and respecting opposing views
Would make a significant contribution to avoiding lighting any short fuse.

Black, White or Shades of Gray?

With attitudes and personalities, does it matter about color or monochrome?
Seeing things in black and white, not exploring with a fine toothcomb
There will be right and wrong, win or lose, with no room for any doubt
Anyone with nuanced views, with you, will have no clout

Once again the specter of uncertainty rears its head
When consideration of possibilities, in between, fills some with dread
It's so much easier to have simple choices
But life is like a choir with multiple voices

Similarly with the rainbow; and even more so with a color chart
With your preferences, you came to a decision, but how did you start
Via the rungs of a ladder or from a cliff to jump or not
All those, in-between, you conveniently forgot?

Art of Defense

Stand up! Be counted! What form should it take?
What is it about and what is at stake
Is there a necessity for an instant response
An attack needing a defense and all at once?

Out of the blue or with time for preparation
Is the need - to justify or seek reparation?
An ideal, under threat from an excess of zeal
Argument or armament - which should appeal?

So many questions, with a need to resolve
Could it be - antagonism, one is able to dissolve
What is the process and is it worthwhile
If you give an inch, will the other party take a mile?

How will you know, unless you at least try?
Why rush in with a whoop and a cry
For some, to talk may seem like a lost cause
But, if it succeeds, one might hear applause

What gave rise to the situation in the first place
Was the other side treated with patience and with grace
Was their desire for dignity and respect plain out of luck
With the sought for compromise, they will now have no truck?

Loss

From the intimate to the distant; the accidental to the unavoidably manifest
From those severely taxing one's wits, to those too small to need conquest
Through extremes of individual loss, to issues for the whole of humanity
Variety, which can hit all of us, in ways which may challenge our sanity

It could be something physical, through carelessness or theft
If it was a bodily or mental attribute we'd be more likely to be bereft
Occasionally ones of intellectual property but, more often, of identity
And one in love or one in death would never be classed as a nonentity

Thinking of issues monetary, it could be from gambling or investments
Or falling on hard times and failing to meet one's financial commitments
Somewhat less tangibly, but equally forceful in terms of the mind,
Are dreams, hopes, aspirations and opportunities, often intertwined

Then there are matters more sensitive, because they are privately depicted
Virginity, deteriorating self-image or sexual capacity sadly restricted
On the larger stage those involving the quality of air, water and food
Those relating to habitat and extinction should also be vigorously pursued

We won't get into the subject of how one can lose what one's never had
But the inability to cope with any of the possibilities may be classed as bad
One doesn't wish to have one's life deteriorate through feeling defeated
Like decisions, success with those minor, with those major to be repeated.

Phobias

Fear - masking a cunning greed
It can have a person running, when it is not what they need
It can precipitate a battle
Even though there is nothing there
It can drive you to the verge of despair

It appears, like a haunting shadow
Even for a French person it is an unwanted cadeau
Go away, take it away - get rid of it!
Such words are a useless fit
It's not so easy, like an involuntary habit

Is there an answer to this cloud on the horizon?
It's like a magnet, as firm as glue
Whatever is one supposed to do?
One tries, one makes an effort, one perseveres
Sometimes the hoped for breakthrough nears
Then hopes are dashed and the cloud never clears

There is an apparent loneliness
And, at times, a feeling of helplessness
An urge to do, or not to do
And still that cursed glue
How to find the will to try anew?

Others are desperate to help
But their kindness doesn't seem to make one's reluctance melt
It's as though there's a communication barrier
Open doors to progress implore
The effects of which go right to the core

The will to win has not gone away
And there is no such word as can't, many say
If it is true, how is the solution to be found?
Even thinking about it makes the heart pound
But determination will eventually pay and those dear, I will confound.

Out the Window

Good gracious, the window's gaping
Don't tell me you've done it yet again
At obeying rules, you're amazing
Which are there, as much for guidance as to be enforced
The need to think, they shouldn't be totally negating
Sometimes the proof is in the breaking
Maybe we've given you too limited a perspective
Where you notice individual pieces of the jigsaw
But the overall picture, you are immune from considering
Is this an indication of your point of view?
A facade we need to cut through
Maybe you close your eyes to potential consequences
Or sometimes even take leave of your senses
Where's your commonsense and what about your attitude?

Swing of the Pendulum

Tick tock; tick tock - like an old casement clock
Never stuck in the middle, always to the extremes it does rock
Tick tock; tick tock - often nothing to do with the time
Surging waves; a tide - in and out; social constructs like a crime

Overcooked for a while; balanced out at the opposite boundary
A propensity to overcompensate on the reverse swing is legendary
Tick tock; tick tock - nothing ever goes one way for ever
When the herd enthuses or is in the depths of despair - be clever

Tick tock   Tick tock

The Little Matter of Money

Water flowing down a river; things not growing on trees
One, effortlessly to deliver; the other, like catching a feather in the breeze
Quality with ease; hardly enough to avoid a shiver
Waste which does not displease; appreciation of a giver

Abundance in the air; a treasure found and treated with care
Grains of sand, lots to spare; appreciation of a treat, rare
Degrees of envy; shades of pity
The provider or receiver of charity; both extremes seen with clarity.

Curse of Growth

The body, the population, the economy are concerns around the globe
The last of these is the one upon which we might point a strobe
There are so many expectations in the direction of growth
But, should it be; have we really given our troth?

The desire always seems to be for a better life, involving materiality
Yet, at the end of the day, what is its effect on each personality
There are a majority, in the world, who could fairly aim in this direction
For the rest, would we benefit from a form of spiritual correction?

Now, we're not about to become involved in some religious squabble
Another subject, for another day; no need, our concentration to hobble
The current trend is for a widening gap and the risk of a dangerous reality
Many of those, with the most, overtaken by greed and lack of morality

To correct this tendency would entail the equivalent of an earthquake
Vested interest dominance is something to which we must be wide awake
With a society, having material calculations, which may not be met
Could it cause serious discord and all sorts of relationships to plummet?

How to find an optimum solution, on the road to a fairer distribution?
We don't need to witness retribution, even less any kind of revolution
Bottom up or top down, but preferably some form of joint resolution
Entailing, from this drug, an obligation to break careless compulsion!

Philanthropy and the Morality of Wealth

Wealthy or beyond but, most likely, the other side of the divide
It varies from culture to culture, but still a phenomenon worldwide
In the bible, Luke 6:38, states "Give, and it will be given to you."
Buddhism refers to enlightened beings being magnanimous givers - true?

But doubt creeps in about the extent of giving in order to receive
It's a common marketing ploy to give and then ensnare; or are you naive?
Sayings such as 'nothing is free' or 'there's no such thing as a free lunch'
Always valid or may there be real integrity when it comes to the crunch

"The Origins of Virtue", by Matt Ridley, is a classic sociobiological book
If you wish to read deeply, it's not one you should overlook
It may well not appeal, it's doubtful you will have such zeal
Assumptions and taking things for granted can be a dangerous deal

When you reflect on the various ways people become wealthy
Do you ever wonder if it may have been by means unhealthy or stealthy?
One person's wealth did not grow on trees but equates to others' poverty
Serious philanthropy needs appraising as to sources of financial property.

Motivation

Beckoning [120] - Motivation

Inspiration

Soaring with excitement, as in a wondrous dream
The rainbow reflects its colors
Raindrops, tears of joy bursting forth in a new-found way
So long it wasn't true, but now
With smiles and song, a heart rising in anthem
Its beat so full of life, enthusiasm rules the day
Thoughts race far and wide and yet
Not in gay abandon, but with purpose to portray
At last you're heading, yes, moving your rightful way
Such a need for great fulfillment, for expression of yourself
It needed perseverance and skill with which to reach
The stars may be far away, the sky is clear
No clouds today to hide their sparkle - it is as it should be
When everything is possible and can't is out of play.

New Beginning

Decisions made and acted upon
Decks cleared, fond farewells
Wishes, friendship and love - given and received
Tears flowed for all to see ....
Others hidden within

Arms reached; lips met
The warmth and closeness of an embrace
Words said and unsaid, the thoughts
Flash across the mind at leaving someone
So many - behind

The pull and push, the past, the future
But here, and now - emotions mixed, changing
Smiles, then watering of the eyes
Tears, then laughter
Voices cracking with emotion

Turning as, back to back, the gap widening
One direction returning to familiarity
The other heading towards such a different future
Uncertain, exciting, challenging - the unknown calls
Unseen magnetic forces cannot let poles remain apart

Pounding of hearts and wheels
Interstate miles, airport files
Anticipation, adrenaline, until
Up above white and fluffy clouds - blue beyond beckons
Exclaiming - new adventure, new beginning

For all the world, a smaller place
So much more difficult to hide; yet distance still a divide
Physical presence so different to email or the Internet
Communications easy to maintain
Reality to create and virtuality disdain

Forward to succeed, but in what way?
Who cares? The mind will win in its own strange way
Who knows what will be achieved who has not tried and cannot win
The fear of loss or the comfort of the status quo cannot be
For those who dare to face the challenge from within.

Motivation

It can emerge or evaporate every day of life, often without permission
Its effects differ when full of optimism or in the depths of depression
It depends on the choices we have and upon which we decide to act
Faced with a deadline it may be easier to find - isn't it a fact?

Within one's abilities, it seems to correlate with one's level of interest
Yet, at the same time, it may be driven by a need, bringing out one's best
It stems from many things - not least love, hate, ambition or an obsession
One strives to avoid regression, by having it in one's possession

The problem arises for those with difficulty finding the necessary desire
As though lack of hope or direction, against their progress does conspire
How do you find it, if your primary needs are not aligned?
Such a contrast to a driven person, who has left basic concerns behind

This suggests existence on several stepped levels; like climbing a ladder
Higher ones, when out of reach, causing frustration and getting madder
Those with least may need education or support for it to be increased
Without it, from difficult or sad situations, they may never be released

There are different ways we can play our part, in aspects of its creation
Whatever its source, the responsibility does not require delineation
The last thing one's wants is to create movement in the opposite direction
Initiation, guidance and resolve - all part of making a mental connection.

Hope and Compassion

One word, in life, you'd never like to lose - which would you choose?
Hope has such an impact - adding optimism and belief to one's views
In the best of times, one most likely takes it for granted
In the toughest, you may wish to have someone else's transplanted

To be a prisoner of especially negative circumstances can lead to despair
How do you appreciate the psychology, if you've never been there?
Compassion can be directed at one's' self; or towards another beneficiary
To know the gift, you give, doesn't necessitate belonging to the judiciary.

Alternative Focus

When mental anguish seems impossible to extinguish
What is the route, the ogre to vanquish?
When distress and despair suggest the mind is beyond repair
Is there a way, to one's self, to be fair?

An almost total eclipse of the original - authentic
Caused by thoughts cycling and distorting - concentric
Where once was a person, there now is a shadow
Needing escape from the maze, to a setting to hallow

A camera with variable focus is worthy of mention
Trained on a landscape where features compete for attention
Choice, at the fork in the road, may be hard to explain
One causes pleasure; the other causes pain

To the left a well-worn track
To the right - overgrown; a way, one would have to hack
A signpost, clear and bold; the other faded and worn
One like a magnet; the other looking forlorn

Deep inside a warning rings
The easier route may be downhill with wings
The other may be like being on trial
But meeting the challenge may be so much more worthwhile.

Advancement and Pushing the Limits

There are certain benefits of basking in reflected glory
However, you may find it more satisfying to create your own story
How would it read and how could you do it
Learning to commit and avoiding the urge to quit?

Small steps can lead to big strides
But will it be you or another who decides?
There's no joy on the road of decline, let alone on the one to being flop
Building one small success on another is a wonderful swap

The first thing to do may be to stop negative thinking
Have a go at something a little large, instead of just shrinking
If you achieve it, you may find yourself, with disbelief, blinking
You will have taken a step up and stopped yourself sinking

Along the way, you could have to go to great lengths
In minimizing weakness and building your strengths
This should be supported by giving yourself options
Choices of which are likely to be the better adoptions

There are other ideas which you may wish to consider
They spring from focus and inspiration and should never hinder
As you progress on the road to disciplining your mind
To the possibilities of conquest you will no longer be blind.

Survival, Escape and Reinvention

A long way we had to trek
It was awful - the car was a complete wreck
How we'd managed to survive, and then escape, was anyone's guess
It left us with a completely new situation to address

I'm sure you've been confronted by something not turning out as expected
You had to be resourceful, after being forsaken and becoming dejected
What does it take to dust off and carry on again
To uplift the mind and, with yourself, strike a new bargain?

Maybe there's a need for reinvention, requiring inspiration
Perhaps accepting a helping hand or some form of mediation
Whether voluntary or not, we can find ourselves outside our comfort zone
But - don't stand still, get depressed or start to moan

It's not always the easiest thing in the world to avoid
But the effort's worth it, rather than plunging into a deeper void
One has to find self-belief, enabling an appropriate correction
Leading to being back on track, heading in a motivating new direction.

Loneliness

Flowering in a sea of wheat - a single red poppy waves
Silhouetted in a sand-dune landscape - a solitary figure craves
In an expansive meadow - a distant oak regally stands
Bobbing on the waves - a one-man canoe, a pair of hands

These may occur naturally or may be sought-after solitude
In other circumstances, an air of unwanted negativity imbued
Such may be a situation in which you, yourself, have found
On occasion - a learning experience; perpetually - like being drowned

Some may bring it on themselves; others, involuntarily crowned
Failure to understand someone lost in a crowd should be downed
In the extreme, the condition can lead to withdrawal into depression
So, provide a little help along the road to more positive self-expression.

Searching the Cloud

Dust devil, tornado, hurricane, tsunami
Shades of nature's version of origami
How can it be; they are so destructive?
What is needed is hope, answers or measures reconstructive

Beyond the horizon, in a calmer place
Thinking minds, with actions, emotions to replace
The challenge of finding a new way forward
Being stoic, finding fortitude, avoiding being a coward

From groups to individual demeanors
To the person who feels taken to the cleaners
Maybe a feeling of something grossly unfair
However one looks at it the problem is still there

Silver linings and opportunities - where
Darkness and defeat stare everywhere
How to turn platitudes into inspiration
How to fight back; restore one's original destination?

Can it be better to travel than arrive
Can one rediscover an essential inner drive
What will it entail, one's spirit to reclaim
A spark of light, in the gloom, to turn into a flame?

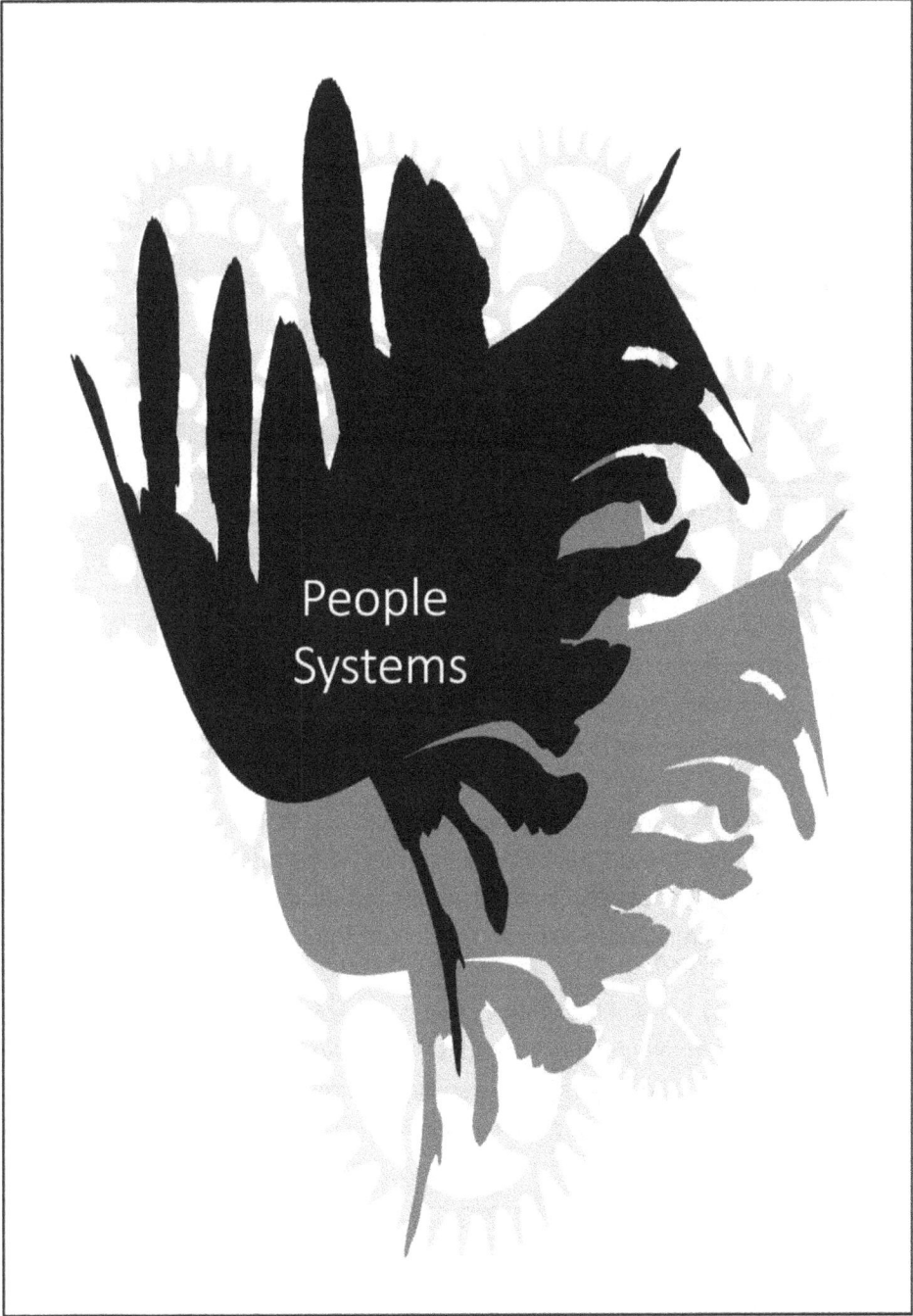

People Systems

Beckoning [131] - People Systems

People Systems

Let's start by clarifying what on earth the words might signify
Anything giving structure to people's lives, their purpose to magnify
At one extreme - education, religion, politics and work ringing bells
At the other - casual groupings, associations, teams, gangs and cartels

All things giving some form and shape to life - for better or worse
We ought to consider whether they fulfill their goals or are ever a curse
How do they impact the extent of real freedom - all over the planet
From being as flexible as possible, to being as hard and tough as granite?

So many people are too busy, with everyday living, to be deep into caring
They don't have time to lift their eyes until something at them is glaring
For example, surveillance is justified as benefitting the vast majority
Street cameras, hacking or security services with a hidden new priority

Of course there are lots of more positive examples, in most people's eyes
Social media and entertainment are the last things they would despise
But there is a huge difference between the developed world and the rest
Where provision of housing, clean water and even food is put to the test

Whatever their quality, we all rely on them, often take them for granted
Smart phones, instant communications, health services never recanted
So easy to accept and unknowingly slide into an insidious comfort zone
Where, maybe without us realizing, the seeds of our own control are sown?

Religion

Does it matter to which religion you subscribe, as long as you sing its song?
It's all about conviction, having faith and knowing why you belong
Will it help to understand, by looking at the definitions of religion and faith?
The former about prodigious creation; the latter a positive form of wraith

A variety from which to choose, some with a different God; few with none
Why they are all different raises questions about the phenomenon?
Even so, each group of adherents attempts to live according to its creed
Doing the will of God, whose superhuman existence, cannot be guaranteed

Humans have a spiritual need to explain the unknown, requiring a belief
It helps to ease the question of life's purpose; its acceptance giving relief
Despite having caused death and suffering across the ages; and still incites
Taking inspiration, love, hope, support and forgiveness to unusual heights

Excluding extremes, those with rational approaches, have immense appeal
Where else is the moral leadership for each generation to strike a deal?
Aspects of mankind's behavior are difficult, if not impossible, to explain
But, regardless, for those who are committed there exists no higher domain.

Religion, Politics and Vested Interests

Pray! Vote! Do nothing by rote
The pensive mind, the political divide
Family traits - through open gates
Certainty and confusion reign
Left and right with all their might

Worship, yes or no, and, if so, how will it show
Spiritual, religious, material
And through what aspects of persuasion?
Still waters run deep
Trying, systematically, to define

How deep is the veneer of civilization
What stops it splitting apart
Sometimes, when it does - does it display the animal in all of us
The interests of the individual or the interests of the people
And which people? Are they ones in whom the interests vest?

What distortions may arise over life and death
Morals; principles; or expediency
Majorities or minorities, approached with too much leniency?
Questions about direction
Often lead to heated words with strong inflection

What causes discrimination?
Why is it still so prevalent?
Race, creed, color, rich, poor and others are still salient
Can white be black or black be white
Sometimes opposites, sometimes the same
Some may think it's like playing a game
For those, at its heart, it's not the way they wish to take part

A desire to rule; a desire to have others conform
To give hope in times of despair, regardless of whether it is truly fair
What is it about corruption and from whence does it get its power
A spin with bias, at times sounding pious?

Non-Political Politics

'Politics is the art of the possible', a British Prime Minister once said
But it wasn't the sort of politics going through my head
My thoughts were on all other forms of organization
Whether run for profit or supported by donation

They come in all sorts of shapes and sizes
From the largest to the smallest enterprises
Managing, to meet their goals, can be full of good and bad surprises
However they are run there will always be a need for certain compromises

Those may be on price or quality and extent of service
But there are people aspects, which could only be dismissed by a novice
There is nearly always some form of unofficial hierarchy or status
So awareness of unwritten motivations may avoid an unpleasant hiatus

One danger is those, appearing to have no real political skills,
May be leaders with the most and, if you knew, they'd give you the chills
However there are many others, maybe most of us to some degree?
How we play the game depending on personality and even pedigree

Are these activities more acceptable if there's some level of mutuality
But a problem, if seen as for personal gain; akin to a form of immorality?
What if two members of the same concern have an unknown relationship?
Siding with one against the other could be dangerous gamesmanship

Where does one go from there, should you care?
Is there some route to playing it clean and, to others, being more fair?
A degree of understanding of those around you, and balking at taking sides,
May be an approach ensuring the entities interest, with yours, coincides?

Alternative Beliefs

Whatever one says or believes, there is always the question of conviction
Is it blind or is it knowing and, anyway, what's the distinction?
What inspired its development and what's its true reason?
Don't forget, there's more than one, so maybe it depends which is in season

If we analyze it, of what do we talk
And how do we choose which way to walk the walk?
There's more to this than meets the eye
Ultimately it can even be believe or die

If a belief is the same as a faith what would hold true for you and I
Surely it can't just be something we would pluck from the sky?
Let's give it a try and see where it leads us
Maybe we'll both find different kinds of buzz

I have faith in myself but there are times when I need faith in a friend
Who such a friend might be could very much depend
What about faith in a machine, driving the Interstate at speed extreme
And, when you sit in a self-drive car, will it take faith of which you dream?

Have you ever had anyone tell you 'You must follow your heart'
In the realms of our discussion would it have pulled you up with a start
Can you reflect on any situation where you have effectively run blind?
Before you do, maybe we should consider something of a different kind

Regardless of anything else, there are only two kinds of belief in the end
Ones on which we may or may not be able to depend
We often reach our own conclusions, but some mean degrees of collusion
With a number of them, we are at risk of becoming victims of delusion.

Population

Onwards and upwards, forever climbing
It's as though there is something needing priming
Physical, yet aided and abetted by aspects mental
Leading to something possibly detrimental

A desire to copulate; a necessity to populate
With angles many fail to postulate
Sustainability is an attractive word
From others, ingenuity may more often be heard

As with water in the desert
Opposing ideas may disconcert
Action, the extremes to avoid
Of opinions or cares devoid

The human race has a propensity to push to every limit
Any excess, only at the extreme, may it act to trim it
It's as though there can be no deprivation
Only an argument between creativity and creation

If it really is the case
Are we all supposed to just stand by and 'watch this space'
Were you never taught to be pro-active
Surely it's the way to find an approach more attractive?

Relative Situations in Life

There are so many differences, spread far and wide around the globe
To which we should give consideration and our reactions probe
About their causes we will not all agree but, their existence, we must see
Some may bring it upon themselves, but to what degree?

Whether you live in a country where capitalism is king
Or in one where, to dictatorship, those in power cling
Which side, of any divide, do you find yourself today
Least fortunate or most fortunate; or perhaps about halfway?

Regardless of your situation, you will be the rare exception
If you have no compassion and indulge in self-deception
It's not purely economics, but values and enlightened morality
Extreme gaps needing narrowing, changing universal mentality.

Comparisons and Contradictions

There are truths and there are fictions - sometimes the source of frictions
Perhaps neither should lead down the road to addictions
But they can both be sources of comparisons and contradictions
Could they ever give rise to meaningful predictions?

Let's stand back and seek a perspective, objective
Despite certain tendencies to be drawn to opinions, subjective
There must be a reason why so many are forever comparing
Are they trying, in some way, their self-image to continue repairing?

If you fail to keep up with the Jones's, how do you know
Does it mean you have a problem with the status quo?
Comments are made about people, all over the world, being the same
Many play to win, regardless, the rest of humanity not in the frame

For some, it's do as I say, not as I do - they talk the talk, but don't walk
Yet, if you told them they were full of hypocrisy, they would surely baulk
Is life such that, although there are so many contradictions
Without comparisons there would be worse afflictions?

Freedom

Do you know what it's like to be in prison
Like a bad loaf of bread which has never risen
To stand on the floor at the other side of the door
Seeking the ingredients for which you implore?

Do you take things for granted
Like the trees your forebears planted
Plus the words you can talk and the avenues you can walk?
Do you mark each of them off with different colored chalk?

How many of them would be green and how many red?
Are there infringements of your life which you hate and wish were dead?
If such be the case, the fight you should embrace
Playing your part to ensure freedoms stay in place.

Control

The hourglass figure enhanced by shape-wear
A horse tethered by a rope
A stop light indicating when not to go
Instruments of detection, leading to inspection
Materials for light reflection
Forces, mental, make the connection
Some would argue they are for protection
Like any line in the sand
Flames of rebellion may be fanned
But, no doubt, for the good of all
Theories of conformity echo around the hall
All these things for the benefit of man
Do they conform to any particular plan
Order, discipline, surveillance - anything you'd like to ban?

Bribery and Corruption

Negative influences, prevalent around the globe
Some may be discernible, others challenging to disrobe
A fact of life or leading to division and untold forms of strife
Are they like stabbing the disadvantaged in the back, with a knife?

What sorts of people do it and are they mainly men
Is it an easy form of selfishness, to do and do again?
And, what about the proportion who profess to believe in religion
Are they deserving of understanding, even if only a smidgeon?

We know it exists at all levels of society
And it's quite evidently a form of impropriety
Is it largely bottom up, or top down?
Do those in authority wear the premier crown?

As with drugs, soft and hard, there's a degree of latitude
But is it something which should really affect your attitude?
If someone abuses power or position for their own gain
What sorts of side-effects have been set in train?

In politics, where should one draw the line with lobbying?
Are some of the activities ones to teach your children to start copying?
There are abuses of discretion; philanthropy, at times, not what is seems
Perpetrators of theft, fraud and blackmail - they go to all sorts of extremes

We could go on, with such things as favoritism and nepotism
But probably the entire subject is one requiring pragmatism
In this era of all-embracing surfing and browsing
Do most of us, from our complacency, need arousing?

Immigrants and Immigration

They may be male or female, adult or child, legal or illegal
Wherever their origin or destination, very few will travel in any way regal
Although many are voluntary, force of circumstances is the real issue
Risks are huge and, protection from exploitation, often as thin as tissue

Who makes the rules, how are they applied and what was their provocation
If Europe and the USA are the main recipients - what's the implication?
If you've nothing to lose because of war, persecution or intolerance
Where do you go to flee life's threats and seek potential furtherance?

There are those with other motives, especially through reasons economic
But, most likely, barely one in a million with incentives gastronomic
For an established person, a new life in a new country is an exciting vision
Someone acting out of desperation has taken a very different decision

Is there any way to achieve universal freedom of movement?
The fundamentals may vary but a major factor is self-improvement
We live in a world with finite resources and where competition is endemic
Where the balance, between cost and benefit, is anything but academic

No action - a decision with consequences; the opposite - with complexity
Running away from reality is no excuse; nor is losing to perplexity
Treating the symptoms, of many phenomena, inhibits treating the roots
Cultural diversity being replaced by homogeneity - oh, to be in cahoots.

Need to be

In the land of the mountains, a cowboy - not me
So close to the border, a lone cowboy is he
The heat of the day, the cool of the night
And, save for an illegal, no one else in sight

What should he do should he come across me?
Should I let him, I'm hidden, perhaps I should run?
This is a place where I should not be
And he, on his horse, heads straight toward me

North of the border - tiredness, hunger and thirst
North of the border - excitement, tension, and fear
North of the border - same landscapes, not culture
North of the border - estoy aqui!

Slum Dwelling

Ponder on the fifteen percent, of the earth's inhabitants, living in slums
What does it tell us about the human race, or maybe your mind it numbs?
The figure also represents about one third of the world's urban population
This is not a speculation but the subject of serious calculation

You will be aware of shanty towns, favelas and ghettos
But have you heard much about them in political manifestos?
They span the globe and are not confined to poor countries
Urbanization enhances the trend of growing municipal tapestries

Some might argue the high densities of people they contain
Save energy and material usage; suggestions you might entertain
They concentrate disease and grievance, wrongdoing and pollution
All passing from generation to generation, like a type of institution

Maybe there is input for future city dwelling
Where stack houses have some influence, the future foretelling
One major problem is the illegal nature of where so many live
Importantly, what actions can build a beneficial alternative?

Malnutrition and infant mortality again raise the question of morality
Not of others, but of you and I, and a need for a changing mentality
Nowhere is the gap between rich and poor more perceptible
Conspicuous consumption; susceptible to becoming unacceptable?

American Insecurity and Anti-Americanism

Is there something about popularity, leading to a sense of security?
For anyone not understanding, could it portray a hint of immaturity?
Perhaps the inverse is something to which one might give consideration
Regardless of whether applied to an individual or a nation?

It can take a lot of thought to imagine being in the others' shoes
Yet it is so important when there could be a lot to lose
What if there are additional factors - creeping, subconscious and insidious
Would they have consequences - unexpected and even highly perfidious?

How do you react when told you must or are forced to conform?
Direct and obvious; but what if unseen stealth your culture starts to reform
How far has American capitalism gone and has it become crazy
Has the line between morals and hypocrisy become notably more hazy?

When the best form of defense is attack
Is it not unreasonable to expect something negative back?
Waters get muddy when the mix is politics and cash
Giving rise to antagonism, largely hidden until it makes a sudden splash

So what is the answer and how can the danger be diffused?
Anyone who thinks it can be done quickly is utterly confused
There are sensibilities, around the world, needing dignity and respect
They may not correspond to your viewpoint but you cannot just reject

Some picture latent pacifism, displaying weakness round every corner,
Not seeing respect as a two-way street, perhaps reciprocated by a foreigner
You might deter, or even frighten, by a show of strength
But when did you last make a real friend by keeping them at arm's length?

Invasion of Privacy

There's a divide between older and younger individuals
On the subject of privacy - very personal yet bereft of manuals
Real or pretend, cameras cover many of our moves
Fingerprinting and iris photos at airports trample, as though by hooves

A platitude - 'If you've nothing to hide, you've nothing to fear.'
Nothing to do with principles, which some of us might hold dear
Equally, on the Internet, nobody can do anything without being recorded
The bulk of the information being analyzed, sold or hoarded

There may be truth in there being positive aspects to these activities
But, if we stop and think, we may not all have the same priorities
There are intrusions done for financial gain or manipulation
And others which authorities would argue might save a nation

This means more is known about us than we can easily elucidate
In a tight corner, may be misread actions, impossible to repudiate
The result of all this intrusion is we are vulnerable on various fronts
The most significant is terrorism; the excuse for everything it hunts.

Taboos

If you mention one, in the wrong company, you'll be sure to lose
But why should it be so and why should you refuse?
How do things, which were once not spoken about, cross the divide
And, until they do, why from them, should one have to hide?

Keeping friends and finding new ones is probably most people's ambition
Who wants to be the person contributing to initiating the transition?
If everyone was the same, nothing would ever change
Our opinions and ideas we'd never rearrange

When you think of one and bite your tongue
There's no chance of anyone, on your words, being hung
Maybe you'll give some serious thought, to the subjects most fraught?
Doing your bit to break the barrier - press the point and don't stop short.

World by Design

With the powers of a dictator, in which direction would you apply them
As an elected leader, of standing, whose actions would you try to stem
A believer in intelligent design, to whom, would you, influences assign
When you consider the world in which we live, what does it enshrine?

There are so many factors at work; it hardly makes one want to smirk
Much less, to react in an instant; it's too serious for a knee jerk
From nature's sublime beauty to extreme man's despicable repulsiveness
Any search for meaning experiences a high level of elusiveness

Plans, aims or intentions and how about drawings or blueprints
If there were, it's very easy to believe there must have been misprints
Looking forward, is it possible to envisage any enhancement
More importantly, to find constructive ways of initiating movement?

The worst can bring out the best, but it's a perverse way of thinking
However, is it how we work - reactive; from being proactive - shrinking?
If there is to be success in ensuring, for everybody, the world advances
Effecting a transformation will involve completely revolutionized stances.

Peace

Whether of the mind or in the world, it is worth the pursuit
Without it, around our planet, the value of life, it must dilute
The very concept is alien to some, causing impacts negative
How to redress the balance brings forth ideas, often tentative

Think of the characteristics displayed amongst those you know
Be honest with yourself - selfish, aggressive, never had a foe?
If no one is perfect, there's a need to temper one's aspirations
Change will be slow, but with effective transitional destinations

It's essential to identify the origins of the current predicament
Without understanding, how can there be a successful medicament?
We know people have different ideas, in so many ways
They spring from upbringing, environment and words a leader says

Counterbalancing these influences needs action, more than debate
They are not things we can or should ever leave to fate
If someone, a group or a country, has a position of strength
It is likely to want to protect it and, to do so, go to any length

Such stances precipitate tensions, leading to behavior destructive
Arresting them from gaining momentum would be more productive
What would it take to defuse such stresses in ways diplomatic
Mutually beneficial solutions, avoiding approaches problematic?

One could lead by example, but risk being seen as lacking in power
Force would be self-defeating; one's hopes would never flower
There are not many other courses of action one could set in motion
 One sure way, to understanding, is communication - not self-promotion.

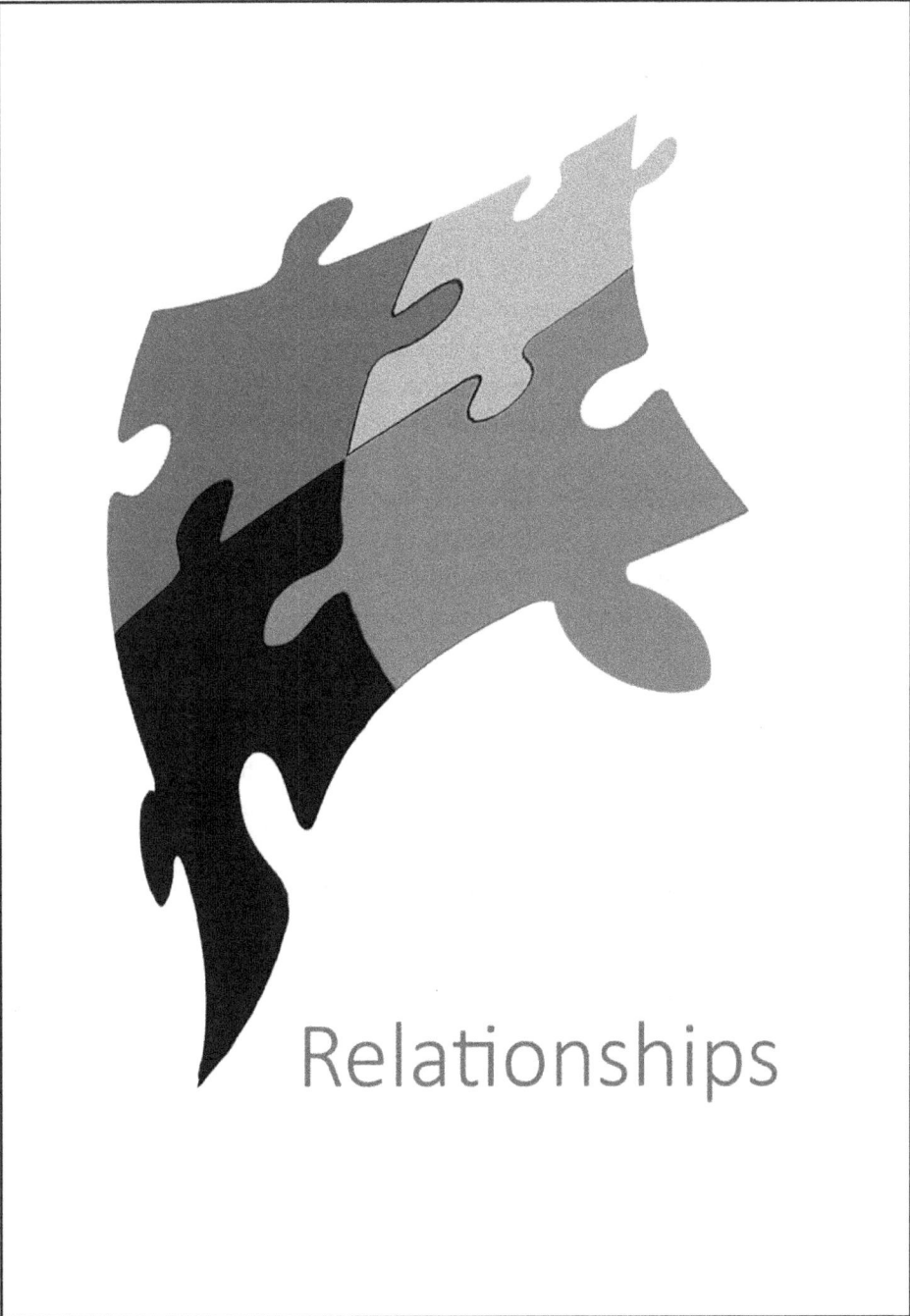

Relationships

Beckoning [151] - Relationships

Friendship

Life, without other people, would be impossible and have no meaning
Mutual support is essential but there are limits, needing screening
It can be easier said than done, when some may not be what they seem
With friends and acquaintances, how do you decide which are the cream?

The decision may be taken out of your hands and spoil your best laid plans
It may not be reciprocated unless you join certain of their clans
True friendship has to be earned; it's not presented on a plate
To presume otherwise might lead you to a disappointing fate

A helpful route involves common interests; especially shared experiences
Painless agreement is all very well, but depth is built on testing sequences
Good times are simple; it's the difficult ones when one discovers the truth
It can get more awkward as one gets older, compared with one's youth

One needs confidence, a degree of trust and a measure of perception
Without, one is vulnerable and a need to be liked opens one to deception
In these days, of overuse of social media, there is an additional danger
Realize the odds, of real friendship, are low every time you meet a stranger.

Loyalty

I never realized it would be a one-way street
How I kept going must have been something of a feat
Giving, giving, giving - asking so little in return
However, at the end of the day, my fingers I did burn

My reference - was to love
When it works, it's like being on the wings of that dove
But when circumstances find the other side of the coin
It ends up like teeth - perpetually drawing

After all the effort, to discover a betrayed relationship
Brought pain beyond any previous level of worship
Life will never be the same again but, despite the loss,
I will not be totally put down and, forever, bear a cross

Now, there are words in the back of my mind
Which I silently think of and hope I might find
Such as trustworthiness, faithfulness, reliability and dedication
Then there's commitment, dependability and, best of all, devotion

Some of these words are similarly inclined
So the balance of importance may need to be refined
Those, whose direction they find ways to address
Will find I reciprocate without the slightest duress.

Open Mind

The shutters came down; the person across the table was wearing a frown
They were supposed to be friends; even came from the same town
Forceful characters, putting it mildly, augmented by some strong views
When they were opposing, one would listen; the other had a short fuse

When singing from the same song sheet - no problem - verging on boring
Now, one was arguing a contrary point of view - the other ignoring
Suddenly a response; but it came with no honestly reasoned arguments
Frustration, intolerance and discrimination rose like fortified monuments

A casual observer would have failed to be impressed
Both were wearing guns - somewhat like the Wild West.
No shots were fired, although there were bullet holes in the ceiling
About what was going on in their heads, it was all rather revealing

Of course, one of the problems is so many people dislike change
And, alteration, for its own sake, could result in reactions strange
To modify one's beliefs gets more difficult the older one gets
A discussion with a critically thinking friend can give one the sweats

Like much in life, it needs time and patience for a solution to emerge
Starting with respect for other opinions, no matter how they diverge
Insecurity, vulnerability and defensiveness - barriers along the road
Discussion of the other's rationale, most likely to be the positive electrode.

Chess

As in life, there are bit players and others who reign supreme
The latter may have weakness, caused by their high level of self-esteem
It can be difficult to knock them off their perch
One may need to do some thinking and preparatory research

There's something about moving forward, even though it can be awkward
Seldom anything to be gained by retreating; it can be self-defeating
However there are situations, leading to alternative evaluations,
When one may force a response by a threat; making the opponent sweat

How big a risk dare one take, especially if it were to prove a grave mistake
If any advantage is lost, how great might be the cost
Can you set a trap, with a good chance of causing your adversary a mishap
If it fails, do you have a defensive plan or will the proverbial hit the fan?

The game will end with a checkmate or resignation
Will it then feel there's been predetermined domination?
The great thing is both players will live to fight another day
What will happen next time and who will win any form of replay?

The Jury is Out

As black meets white, shades of gray come into play
When mediation, is replaced by arbitration, a loser walks away
How arbitrarily are judgments made
Could there be a price which may have to be paid?

Yes or no; on or off can lead to a state of standoff
Progress to resolution halted by the parties deciding to back off
A dangerous moment which could lead to a fight
When a return to talking needs patience and serious mental might

From facilitated compromise a better solution may arise
For those with binary minds, this might come as a surprise
But banish such thoughts for a little while
Fresh ideas of a different kind, in the mind to file

For a person with pride, the effects of ownership can influence
Bringing care and satisfaction into confluence
No dichotomy or contradiction
Winners and losers become a fiction.

Helping Hand

Ever needed a helping hand; but been so proud, you've turned it down?
It's the sort of thing for which people, with good values, have renown
It could also be related to preferring to learn from one's own experiences
Especially concerning things we action, whilst enjoying audiences

One needs care because they can come in various guises
The best are heartfelt and genuine; the worst containing nasty surprises
Family, friends and good Samaritans need no explanation
Do-gooders, meddlers and outright imposters can be a lethal combination

The subject can be treated as two sides of the same coin
Givers and receivers; even winners and losers one can enjoin
The person who wants to be nice and may be imposed upon
Or the altruist operating through enlightened self-interest, never letting on

Some deceive, with crocodile tears, in order to find support
They're not exactly the most difficult to recognize or thwart
If you have the capacity, there's nothing better than relying on one's self
When the need is there, being able to pick it up, off the shelf

As one goes through life, building solid relationships can be so productive
Even a person, far way, electronically connected and instantly constructive
Saying "As I think of you, across the miles, an extended hand you see
Proffered with love, to aid your revival - because you mean so much to me."

Brutality

Has it changed across the ages or is it basically still the same
Manifested differently, but with equivalent reasons and comparable aim?
Does it originate, at the basic level, with mankind's animal impulses?
A question which, because of our veneer of civilization, so easily repulses

Nevertheless, it does not make the subject one we can easily reject
Pursuing perpetrators is necessary, but it's the causes we need to correct
Such is where the real problems lie and should come as no surprise
If we could solve those issues, imagine what the result implies

Some gain or benefit is the intimidator's real target; whatever the form
Regardless of being realistic or imagined; local or causing a national storm
Bullying, burglary and theft; rape, ritual, self-harm, murder and execution
Suppression, torture, terrorism and novel threats - all requiring solution

Reducing or eliminating the factors, giving rise to their precipitation,
Will be much more effective than punishment or exhortation
How this can be achieved has no easy answers but, if no attempt is made,
No end, to this most negative human characteristic, will we ever evade.

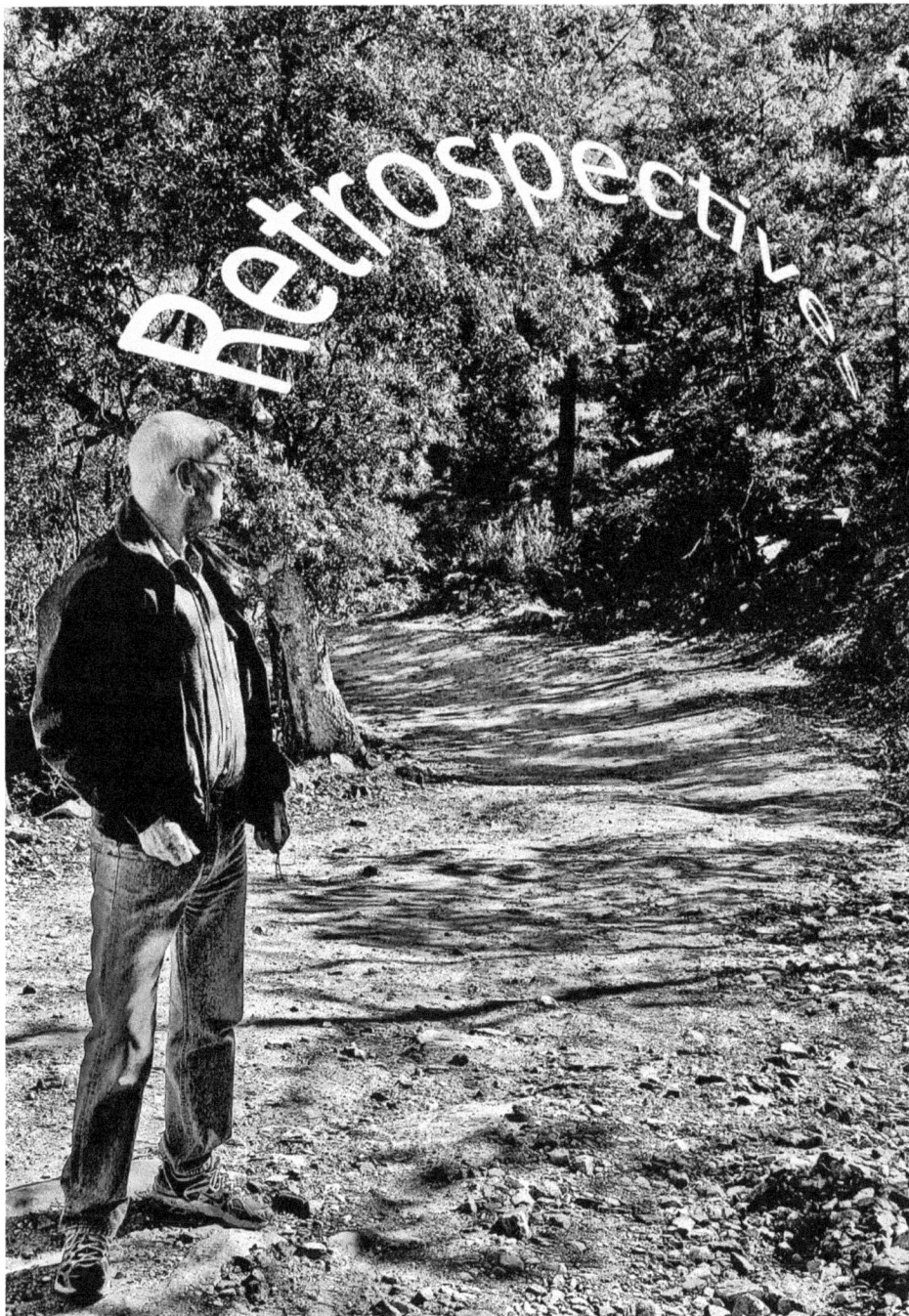

Beckoning [159] - Retrospectives

Retrospectives

Somewhere behind, or was it in the past
It would take a major quirk to make time travel work
Memories, mirrors and possible distortions
The consequences of gilded lilies
Distant shimmerings in the desert
How good was yours; how good was mine?

Lessons learned or overlooked
Changes made; regrets which don't fade
Sorrows gone but still their shadows linger on
Contentment sounds across the meadows
Hidden, over the hills and far away,
Reflections on the same or an alternative way
It matters not, who would give a jot

Not so fast; everyone needs to be put on the spot
Especially when there were others, who've been affected a lot
Past, present, future all combined
Generations come and go
Others reap some of what you sow

Would there still be time to redress the balance
Should haste be made to take the chance - other lives to enhance?
Learn from history, which encompasses good and bad
Strengthen positives; weaken negatives
Give. Don't take. Help others avoid such a mistake.

Aging and Retrospection

With a hoped for inevitability, a duo start to stir
One may cause wondering and the other memories to reoccur
Earlier generations and their place in history
What yours will be is probably something of a mystery

The record, of this famous pair,
May lead to different degrees of expectation and care
Which will come first and how will they be intertwined
Their effects to be distilled or possibly refined?

Like a marriage, with good and bad,
With times of delight, but also some making one sad
The balance doesn't change merely by chance
Nor does it help to make a song and a dance

As with life, these years cannot be repeated
But an imbalance of the two can be defeated
There is a time and there is a place - for both
Still, only to one do we all give our troth

The second comes naturally, from time to time
However, to give it too big a share may well be a crime
Its need to be controlled is not always apparent
Yet the way it can be overplayed should become transparent.

Rearview Mirror

Looking over one's shoulder or turning to confront what is behind
What will you or your conscience see and find?
It may be something of a difficult question
So its ramifications may need time for digestion

Thoughts collected; lines drawn in the sands
Missed opportunities or ones taken with both hands?
The aging process takes no hostages
But retrospection can produce rare sages

Tricks of memory and time, as you flick through the pages
Inconsistent measures or reliable gauges
Too late for changes and maybe even for amends
Can you live with the consequences of the message your life now sends

Your health will, likely, not be what it was
And your changed looks - well, you know it's because .....
Even at this late stage don't dwell on the past
Your future shortens and you need to move fast.

Old Age

The latter part of life - known as advanced or declining years; or senility
Is when you should accept life as it is; and find 'a sense of purpose' ability
There are so many things in its favor, despite knowing its conclusion
And in spite of any health problem making an unwelcome intrusion
Don't be old before you time; try to be youthful regardless of age
It helps if you visualized your latter years, before you reached this stage
Keeping up an exercise regime, both physical and mental
Looking after your fitness and stress levels; to yourself being gentle
These, and socializing, are all elements helping to smooth the way
And, in aging well, they are also matters it's hard to overplay
There are many in the same situation, who still have much to contribute
To have empathy and do so, by volunteering, is a wonderful tribute
With more time for loved ones and, surprisingly, a happier point of view
By, whatever measure, a sense of accomplishment is a fulfilling adieu.

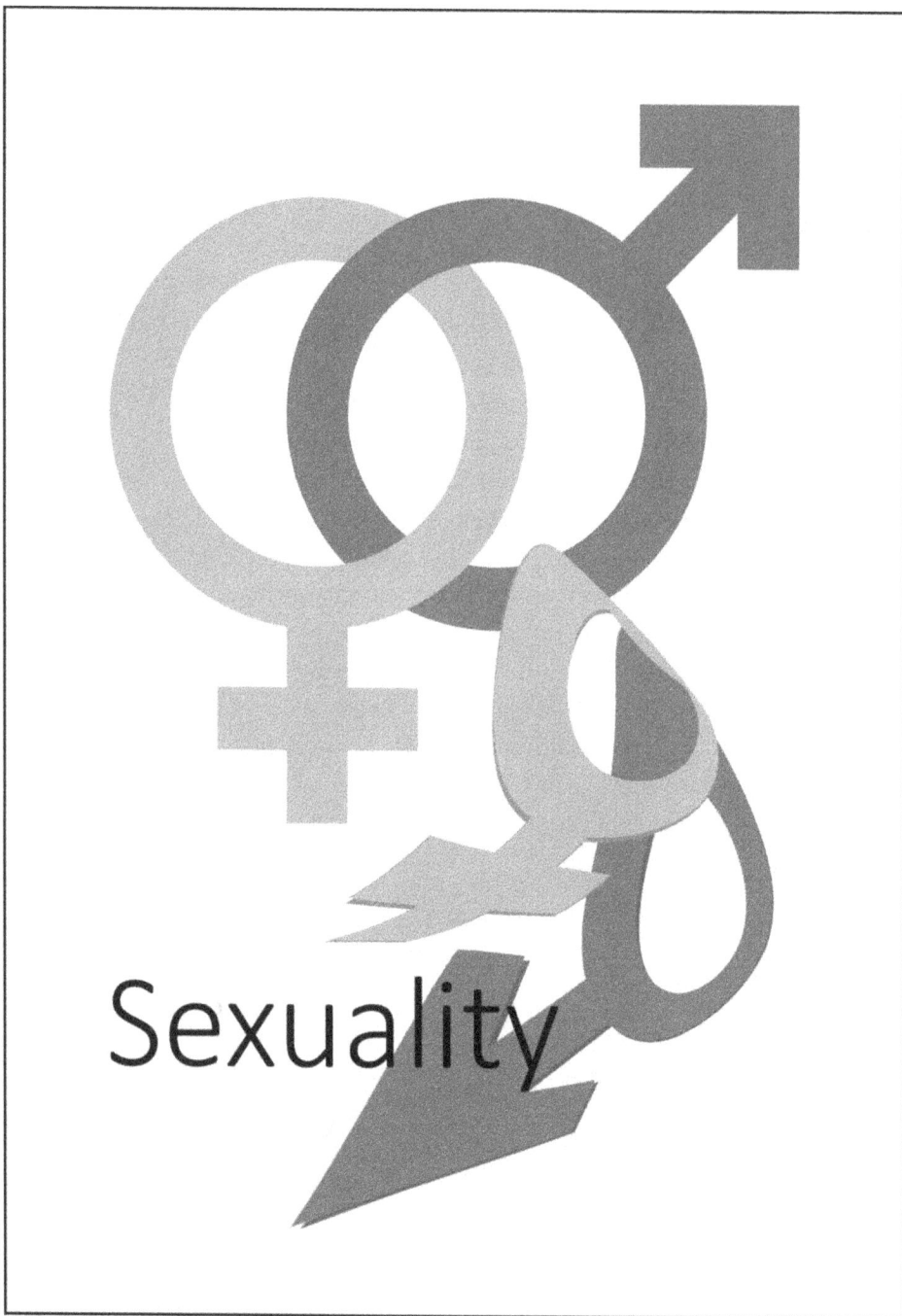

Sexuality

Sexuality

To some extent, most individuals are aware of their own
Although they may have secrets and aspects they hide or disown
How does one discover one's true nature and preferences
Especially if brought up with a strict code of references?

At the extremes, aiming for celibacy or overtaken by promiscuousness,
Both run the danger of going astray; even to the point of deviousness
Let's not dwell on those and, instead, consider healthy evolution
But with no absolution from accepting the curve of a normal distribution

Activities in life, of which it's possible to have too much of a good thing,
Benefit from abstinence; self-control a quality to which one should cling
Over one's life, there's a rise and a fall and varying forms of presentation
Work towards making sure you have no reason for moral lamentation.

Intimacy and Sexual Feelings

Please, do not invade my space
And, certainly, never touch my face!
The time, the place, the person
There needs to be a compelling reason

A special touch and a hint of flavor
Enveloping, with a seductive aroma to savor
The waiting, the anticipation of what one might wish could last forever
Instinctive, but with a degree of endeavor

Distance can compound and lead to reactions profound
But absence may not make the heart grow fonder
Abstinence may make the mind wander
Then, a battle royal may ensue, when one's loyalties test a person true

For most a definitive sense of male or female
Yet, for some, a different hormone balance, adjustments may entail
Then again, intimacy may be derived through sport, adversity or work
It's of a totally different kind and may be stumbled upon, perhaps as a perk

There are aspects, positive and negative, rejecting or being rejected
Memories of a last physical encounter and what to have expected
Climax or anti-climax, connections with pain and pleasure
Missed opportunities to reflect on, at one's leisure

The heightened awareness, at the peak of romance or in a liaison illicit,
Cannot be maintained in an ongoing relationship, which should be explicit
Still there are deeper meanings to which one should have an inclination
As time goes by, changes imply redefinition of your cherished destination.

Equality of the Sexes

As you stand on a soapbox, to pronounce on this subject,
What sort of image do you wish to project
Would it include aspects of individuality you wish to protect?
I'm sure there would also be differences you would want to correct

Your views may be colored, like light through a prism
Yet there could be seeds of change you'd like to sow to escape schism
Some divergence is impossible to alter
Although I suspect the delivery, of your diatribe, would never falter

Certainty is a wonderful thing and goes hand in hand with confidence
If others, with an alternative perspective, agreed - what a coincidence
So, let's work on the basis of particular qualities deserving prominence
Which is not to say specific interpretation should display dominance

With rights protection there is always potential for reverse discrimination
One usually thinks of women's rights; but those of men have fascination
There's inconsistency - each approached from a different perspective
Once more, it's a question of being objective or shaped by the subjective

To cause further complication, neither men nor women have a united view
Touring the world, one also finds other cultural traditions one can't eschew
The sum, of all these diverse opinions, demands a solution evolutionary
There's no one answer, so beware of promises revolutionary

To compare and contrast, then agree or disagree, are strongly hominine
Everyone needs to be flexible whether in a role masculine or feminine
In all walks of life, respect for others' priorities should hold the key
But it only works if we appreciate we're dealing with a sexual potpourri.

Sexual Conundrum

For good or bad, life is nothing if not interesting
It has challenges; it has the unexpected
But what if the unforeseen is rather close to home
Try relaxing and letting your mind roam

Where would it take you and what would you find
If it was something abnormal, could you still be kind
About a loved one, whom you hold dear
Would it cause fear, or a tear; or perhaps put your mind out of gear?

If gays and lesbians are not negatives on your agenda
How about transvestites, transsexuals and transgender?
If the subject was cross-dressing
Would you find it depressing?

To tell or not to tell is a serious battle
Which should it be and whose cage would it rattle?
Some state - to tell is selfish
Others say - not telling is cheating
This gives rise to a conundrum fiendish
The need for a decision, without anyone mistreating.

Coming Out

It began and ended, but the experience was too short
Like a good meal - left needing more and perhaps a glass of port
What a bore to be back where one started out
Envisaging it more complete and prolonged, better than without

Physical and mental aspects enhancing a needy disposition
A volcano rumbling, before expressing a fundamental mission
A new revelation of personality, with an air of individuality
A true manifestation but, hopefully, not of immorality

A touch eccentric, a degree unusual or a shock in certain quarters
Acceptance may be easier than anticipated; but how about supporters?
There's something very difficult about this level of doubt
When one is faced with considering and deciding to come out.

Space

& Beyond

Infinity and the Infinitesimal

It seems both extremes are the same
They happen to be opposite ends of the same game
How can it possibly be
When they are both impossible to see?
However big, however small
There is always something, beyond, which will forever call
Yet there are ideas to which we cling
We think of nothing and everything
For some people this may be a subject they'd rather avoid
But, for others, the challenge can be enjoyed
For certain minds, an interesting test
Two intangible concepts, the basis of their quest
There's one of me and there's one of you
However, at the ends of this spectrum, it is not true.

Dimensions

Aspects or facets will crack open this door
But more than four can become a bore
Attributes of life can readily exceed such a score
What do they mean and where can they be found
Hanging around or going to ground
Then there's the mystery located beyond time
Taxing certain minds, when they are in their prime
Onto something or stringing us along
To which school of thought do you belong?
Could one be right and the others wrong?
Searching for a theory rationalizing the whole
Predictions generating scientific observation being the goal
Have you got to a point where you'd like a translation
Or maybe you need a conceptual demonstration?

Nothing Revisited

Once upon a time, in a place no one will ever know
A happening, with consequences which weren't exactly slow
Yet, boundless time has helped to try and define
An ever-expanding sphere of influence, theories to refine

Nothing, origins, evolution; the future to be foretold
Extremities of scale and time needing ideas bold
Forces, weak and strong; and extra dimensions have strung along
Facts from fiction, a degree of truth, elements of which may be wrong

Once the belief was the world was flat; and what became of that?
The LHC, beyond Higgs Boson, the latest incarnation of the distiller's vat
It raises the question of when is something so small it's actually nothing?
A circle of exploration, under the Swiss/French border - ideas frothing.

Quantum Effects

Is it better to be Jekyll and Hyde or somewhat bipolar
When it comes to this strange world with a unique controller?
It defies all normal logic and can stop you in your track
Concerned at your chances of getting a dead or alive cat back
Of course it may depend on how you go about finding out
Light passing through a dual slit gives rise to even greater doubt
Perhaps your cat will turn into particles or rise with waves
These considerations perform as manifestations of its slaves
Leaping to the other side of the universe may be perverse
But it all so entangled, about it, we really ought to converse
Where to start and where to end could drive you round the bend
With its superpositions, yet something else with which to contend
Anticipate new forms of computing, data storage and cryptography
Extreme, but just imagine the impact of teleporting on cosmography

Been and Gone - A Previous World

When plates move the last thing one needs is to be near a groove
When the big one arrives will it be too late to move?
Taking a vast step, from the future to way in the past
Things never stay the same and change can come fast

Dinosaurs came and went and the earth's energy is far from spent
In a sense, almost endless time for the forces to vent
Greater strength than today, finding ways to dissipate
The earth's mantle, violent in ways one cannot imitate

Periods of almost unbelievable calm
When civilization could develop with little in the way of harm
A world, wearing a different face, may have vanished without trace
How on earth could such a transition have taken place?

How much imagination does it take to contemplate
And why would the world's whole population have met its fate?
If they didn't, there should have been some history to recount
Some hint of an explanation to try and mount

Could the cause have been tectonic activity
For which the earth has an ongoing proclivity
Or perhaps a scenario of a world encapsulated in intolerable heat
Something, even with superhuman effort, impossible to defeat?

Mysteries of Space

Out in space, unexplained forces, each with a different face
It's where dark matter and dark energy both find a place
What are they about and how do we find out
There's so much we don't know, giving rise to doubt

There's talk of a vacuum and a power pushing everything apart
If the opposite was true, would it pull you off your chart?
At this point, it may be worth considering cosmos and universe
The same or different - their definitions seem a bit perverse

To avoid confusion, let's use cosmos to encompass literally everything
With our visible or observable universe something it is bequeathing
Taking this approach, we can then ask where did the forces originate.
Was there something before the Big Bang which might still predominate?

Some might suggest, quite forcibly, the influence of God
Others may, equally, suggest it was a different lightning rod
This is a discussion we will save for another day
The way we are going, we should let other thoughts have a say

The entire subject has prompted many a book
However, in this poem, we can do no more than take a cursory look
The concept is an all-encompassing sphere, and a center of the whole
With an enveloping, uniform extensional force in the leading role

The resulting scenario - one of everything being pulled, not pushed apart
A very different position, from which the development of theories to start
If we postulate our Big Bang not having been the first
It would require others, about which we must be better versed

Possibly separate universes, going in many directions from the original
Taking ours, from being the major focus to being fairly marginal
As such, how do we know where, in the cosmos, our universe is placed?
A new basis from which dark matter and dark energy may be traced?

Space Calls

The amazing world of communications
Connecting people; connecting nations
The inquiring mind may be one of a kind
But, out in the cosmos, what else might one find?

There can be something unsettling about a one way street
Things going the other way which never meet
A desire to encounter; a wish to greet
To make it happen would be a ground-breaking feat

From humanity to others out in space
From space to earth, could there be anything to trace?
There may be many who prefer not to know
Yet others, re aliens, will say "I told you so"

What other forms of life could the universe produce
What form of communication might be in use
Friend or foe and how would one know
Offense or defense - which face will show?

Primitive life forms may be all very well
Advanced may be friendly or like creatures from hell
Having taken a path there will probably be no turning back
From the possibility of each other's code to crack

The desire to achieve is like a mental form of greed
But the cerebral nature of man drives the urge to succeed
The odds are rather long, so let's not pretend
There is no way of knowing how such things would end.

Earth - as Seen by Aliens

Look! There it is - the place sending out SETI signals
The inhabitants seem to believe they're authentic originals
They've a long way to go to emulate our all seeing, all knowing species
To be fair, though, they have inquiring minds, and some novel theories

Yes, but what are they about and why do they think they exist?
It's an excellent question; we could give their minds a good twist
We don't need to, but let's make a quick circuit of their terrestrial home
It won't take long and there may be the unexpected for our historical tome

Just as we knew, see - there, there and there, huge conurbations
Built near fault lines and even more of them down at zero elevations
Is it some way of controlling their ever-expanding population?
They don't seem to care about the long-term, too much of a tribulation

Some do have a longer-term view, but they tend towards dictatorship
Coupled with which they also tend to practice more forms of censorship
There's such insecurity; some national governments going as far as spying
Their history of wars and cut-throat competition - not the least edifying

People consumed with winning or losing; for many, not of their own choosing
There's such a gap between wealth and poverty - like a form of abusing
Many know what should be done, but too selfish for their own prescription
Like global warming; water control will breed resentment and proscription

In their eyes, they do have a history of having progressed
But they don't seem to accept the ways in which they've regressed
Look at the state of deforestation, along with the state of each ocean
Plus, the water's rising and the air above has various degrees of pollution

A saying 'Prevention is better than cure', they sometimes implement
But, more often, they find a last minute fix, then considered magnificent
They're running out of time to put things right by normal human evolution
If they don't come to their senses, it will be a world heading for revolution

They have this facade of what they call civilization
Where there is little kudos for honesty, but plaudits for manipulation
They have the pursuit of what they call happiness, in their daily grinds
They don't seem to realize they'd be better off seeking contented minds

They all need enlightenment and ability for continuous compromise
OK, I've seen enough - let's go! I'm not sure what it might all epitomize
It's as well they can't detect us; otherwise what questions would it raise
We'll be back, in the future, perhaps to witness a redemptive phase?

Beckoning [179] - Space & Beyond

Universe - from Big Bang to a Corresponding Future

Any event, prior to the Big Bang, is an interesting subject in its own right
We're not going back, so far, hence there's no need to take fright
Nevertheless it's a long time since our universe began
Going forward, as far, computes to more than a 25 billion year span

How on earth can one summarize such a passage in a few stanzas?
It's hardly likely to become the best of extravaganzas
Yet the energy already expended, on creation and destruction,
Leaves one awe-inspired at the nature of this cosmic production

For those alive today, testing our minds, what might we honestly say?
Such fleeting observers; yet some degree of understanding we portray
We study its past and present; make predictions as to its future
Yet, so far ahead, can we truly foretell the nature of any conjuncture

The concept of a spherical earth dates from Greek philosophical thinking
Consider the changes in human life since - astronomically, time blinking
Even so, we can't help but study, analyze and wonder
But, despite evolution, we'll never steal the ultimate future's thunder.

View from the Center of the Cosmos

An unobstructed view in all directions
Evidently nothing there, for eons, with which to make connections
Yet, at least light years in the distance
Hints of objects one needed technology to enhance

Unseen, somewhere out there, in space
An apparent void, a unique place
With a specially developed, all seeing, vision
A perforated spherical shell, seen with a degree of precision

Not still, but spreading as it moved away
One could tell - hidden forces were at play
Looking to the farthest reaches, across distances vast
A realization - the multitudes would not last

Into darkness, beyond such a populated zone
Which nothing apparent had yet claimed as its own
It was not a tangible sphere, but one of darkness with special effects
The perforations weren't holes, they were illuminated objects

Three dimensions of universes contained in an intermediate band
As though sandwiched between the push and the pull of a superior hand
The totality of the cosmos; a sphere, inside a sphere, inside a sphere
Observed in this dramatic, but conceptual manner, becomes so clear!

Bio
Construction
Communication
Cybernetics
Energy
Micro
Nano
Space
Transportation
Water

Technology

Electronics, Internet and Social Media

Is there no limit to the ever-increasing speed of communications?
Regardless of the answer, there are already interesting ramifications
Do you remember the bookworm, he's not yet extinct
In fact, despite everything, he's developed quite a survival instinct

Smartphones; and tablets, so unlike those of stone
With their mobility, changing the world; much like a cyclone
You may or may not have heard of tribes, but you will have self-selected
Thinker, searcher or leaper - a price for being socially connected

What are the effects on society - both as a group and an individual?
An important question, when the last thing one can say is they are gradual
Most users would say the benefits outweigh the disadvantages
However care needs to be taken not, to the future, to be hostages

There's a considerable divide between adults' and one's children's use
From various perspectives there is a lot of potential for abuse
Generally, cyberbulling refers to children and cyberstalking to adults.
No escaping; online hurt or embarrassment may magnify harmful results

Sext-reposting, flaming and illicit tagging may trigger social exclusion
Impersonation and identity theft can lead to a most exasperating conclusion
Milder things like a deficit of body language and social context
And the question of a surfeit of information, regardless of the pretext

To finish on a more positive note would get my vote
You could hardly call the subject in the least bit remote
Maintaining and developing connections, social and business, stand out
Education, employment, life quality and global issues gain added clout.

Information Overload

Imagine telling the wood from the trees, when already lost in a crowd
On top of that, the music was deafening, as you onward ploughed
The deadline was fast approaching and a decision needed to be made
So much information; there was no way it could all be weighed

It was reminiscent of the NSA - the more they got, the more they wanted
Increasing processing power, developing new algorithms - undaunted
Social media is in play but, access to one's privacy, loosely voluntary
Distinct from search engines, seeking profit from underhand commentary

Yet there are so many benefits, despite the manipulation of Big Data
Communication and research facilities make it difficult to be a hater
Nevertheless there is a burden, potentially causing imperfect application
Sometimes the result of what can be known as infobesity or infoxication

But let's put privacy to one side, to be addressed again on another day
Survival and efficiency in the information age are ideas we should convey
We ought to address cognitive overload and information paralysis
Use of time and being permanently connected - subjects for analysis

Praise of multi-tasking has been shown to be a concept we should dismiss
Not to cite time management, self discipline and control would be remiss
Most important, may be to take a break - making filter to focus the norm
Almost impossible to achieve unaided - time to consider crowd reform?

Robotics and Automation

Are fears, of the former's increasing use, irrational and unfounded?
Automation doesn't cause the same concern - adaptability confounded
Perhaps, more interesting and provocative, collaborative robotics
Wrongly developed, may increase the use of narcotics
Just imagine what could go wrong with artificial intelligence
Learning from mistakes being applied with defective diligence
In an intertwined working environment, machine and man,
How fail safe would be any emergency contingency plan?
Nevertheless, progress will be effected, complete with advantages
Hopefully, in its realization, there won't be too many hostages
Especially, as there will no longer be a need for safety cages
Perhaps this will be ensured by rules by which each party engages?
There is one essential electronic device which must be in place
Knowing when to call for human intervention, in its knowledge base.

Time

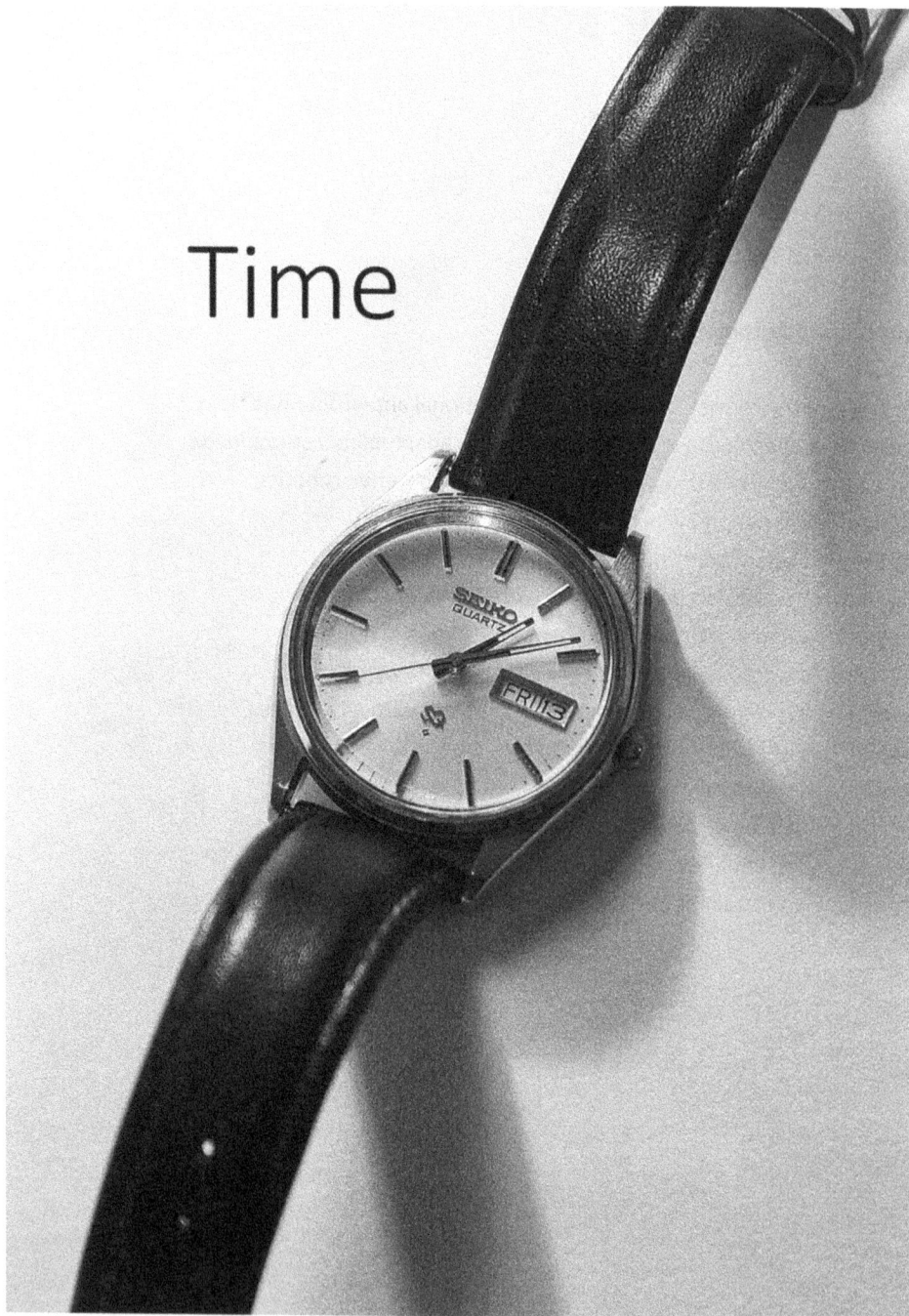

Beckoning [186] - Time

No Time like the Present

You must have noticed everything becoming the past - sometimes too fast
Even the future, when it arrives, no sooner here than gone, into history vast
We have dreams and memories but the present is always here
There's a saying 'Live for the moment' to which you might yourself endear.

Time for Action

Dark, yet discrete, the clouds scurried across the deteriorating sky
Purely incidental to a situation which could be do or die
Now was the time and this was the place
Earlier difficulties, not relevant to the stakes for which I was about to play

Thoughts came and went, and then returned
Memories flashed and my stomach could have churned
Plans made and then revised; and then revised again
No longer a question of if; and, if so, how

The reality was upon me and there was no turning back
Never a perfect time and there may be subsequent mountains to climb
Now, as the elements competed for attention
There was no longer room for any pretension.

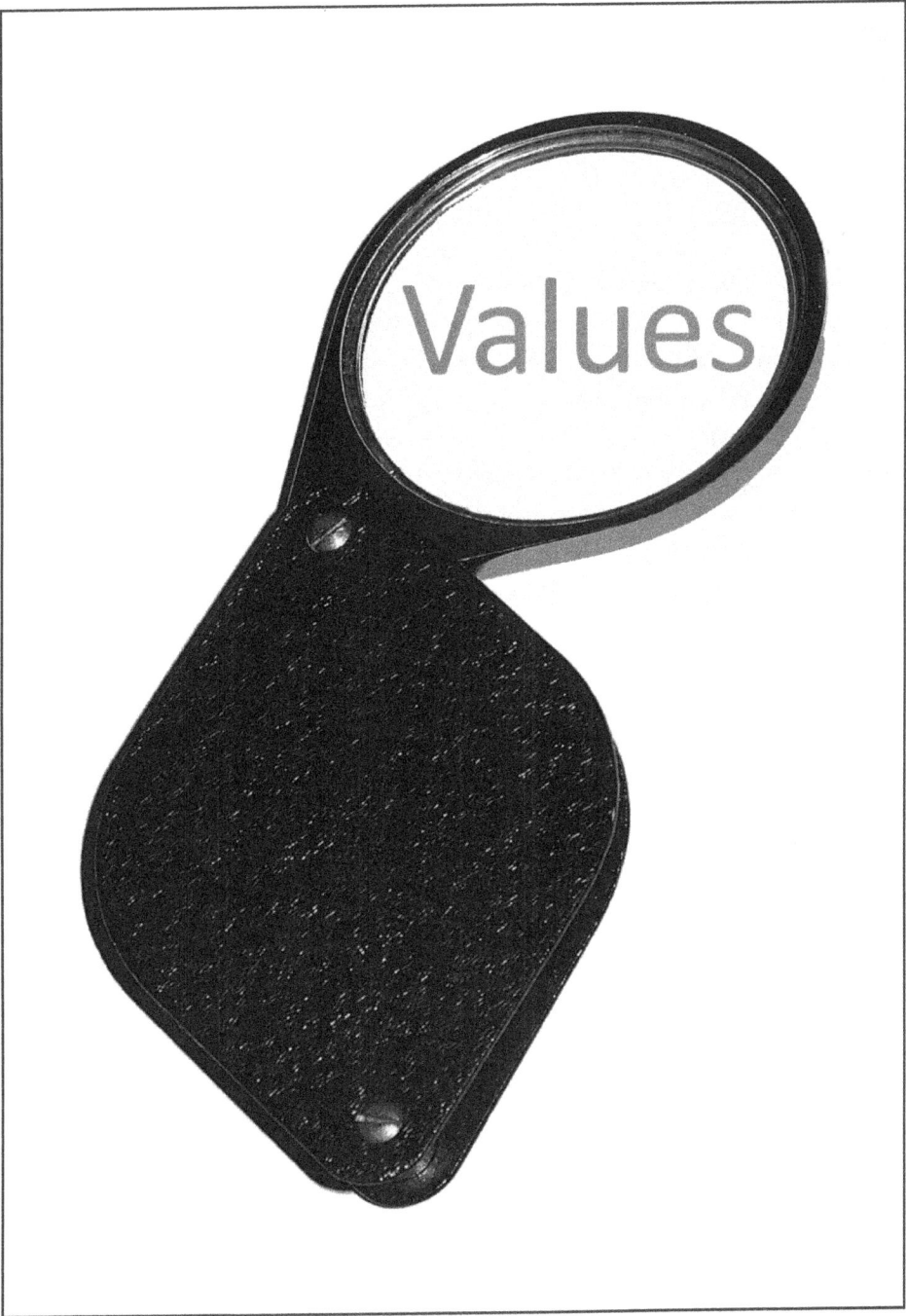

Beckoning [189] - Values

Alternatives

Every time you make a choice, it's because you are faced with alternatives
Their consequences shape your life; be they positives or negatives
They may be obvious and easy; but the best may need some teasing out
Even when you've unearthed them, they may take effort to bring about

They can be opportunities, some of which will never be repeated
If you miss them you may have regrets, or suffer from feeling cheated
It could be more complicated - added risk or negation of a comfort zone
How to recognize such an instance could be an important stepping stone

Unless there's no choice, closing doors or ditching options is inadvisable
Boxed into a corner is a weak position and may lead to a problem sizable
So imagine the difference made by, of the better ones, taking advantage
No one is always totally right; it's a case of maximizing one's percentage

Regardless of whether talking education, relationships or life priorities
Or subjects like finance, spirituality, self-image or lifestyle minorities
Of all the alternatives, presented or created by one's own choosing
Confusing, amusing or made for refusing - always try to avoid losing.

Challenges and Decisions

Which choice would it be - decisive challenges or challenging decisions?
There is a difference, but it may depend upon one's values and visions
One suggests a binary outcome; the other a plurality of situations
However, they could stand alone and embrace other applications

'What's life if it's not problems?' a wise man asked, words chosen with care
He took me aback - so negative, almost made it sound like a nightmare
Later, I found myself thinking the comment was actually profound
I decided to substitute challenges - it was a better word, in the round

A more constructive word, which influences one to rise to the occasion
All it needs is a decision and a degree of preparation
Sometimes one is tempted to put off decisions, especially when demanding
It can lead to procrastination and trigger the need for reprimanding

Both come in different sizes; from insignificant to downright scary
However they play on the mind, the way one reacts is sure to vary
It's not hard to realize these words can give rise to the same trait
Accepting a challenge or making a decision - reflections in a portrait.

Materialism

Value! Meaning! How many objects can one unearth?
Stuff to acquire which makes one feel one's worth
Could it be an illusion; maybe even lead to confusion
Or perhaps be ignored and lead to profusion?

The depth of this subject is more than skin deep
And, if seriously considered, raises the question of what one should keep
But what is essential and what is definitely not?
Surely, if the later, it should not be left to rot?

What should one do, to one's self to be true?
Is the answer so difficult to bring into view
Are there obvious or hidden influences at work
Essential quality of life or some kind of perk?

What one has never had, one never tends to miss
The reverse may be like the consequences of a special French kiss
All around the world, the extremes are unfurled
From some quarters, not unreasonably, insults could be hurled

Can there be a balance, when there isn't a bottomless pit
The urge to acquire, justified by reason and with wit
Scruples, conscience, fairness - how can they be measured
To what extent should the idols of matter be treasured?

Chancing Your Luck

Did you take a chance, calculate a risk or completely count on luck
Whichever you approach you took, did you win or come badly unstuck
I wonder what you thought the odds were - sufficient to roll the dice
Was your confidence such you thought it was worth the price?
But, then perhaps you had no option - you had nothing to lose
When you have so little there appear to be no other avenues
Have you ever applied this to mega lotteries and their immorality?
Those, who really can't afford, treated with disproportionate brutality
In the extreme, what control did you have when born into this world
Fortunate or was it like, onto a slippery slope, being hurled
Can luck be good or bad; things happening by accident or chance
Can you count on such things, your life to enhance
If not, what can give you hope for some form of escape
Is it impossible, without society's help, to avoid moral and financial rape?

History

To some people history is something of a mystery
For others, they'd have a preference for discussing upholstery
Such persons might even discover a stitch in time, saves nine
Yet what would they know about civilizations, past and their decline

Enthusiasts look at it in a totally different way
More than academic interest, to lessons learned having a future say
Not to dictate actions, which should be taken
But, as far as possible, to forestall doing things mistaken

We, as mortals, each have a history, evolving each and every day
Our collective memories, properly sorted, historical knowledge portray
This applies to all human groups, including characteristics less tangible
When anyone is negative, tell them, for a place in history, they are eligible.

Truth

Does it really matter what language is used
Can it be absolute or its meaning abused
One for me; which may not be for you
If such is the case, what can one construe?

Moving targets can prove difficult to hit
Deep discussions may fall into a bottomless pit
The passage of many moons can unearth new facts and paradigms
Making what was valid, appear like a dinosaur, from earlier times

Nevertheless, all over the world, the searchers continue
Ardent followers straining ever sinew
Searching with purity, complete with lucidity
For the proof, ensuring eternal validity.

Two Concluding Poems
1. Taking a Ride   *The author's life*

Taking a Ride

A degree of risk
At a pace, quite brisk
How would it be manifest
And would it stand the test?
An occasional stir, perhaps, but never a whisk

Long days, weeks, months and years
Yet, flashing decades, nine lives, like cat's purrs
From womb to grave
Would there be anything to save?
It did seem, quite likely, he'd earned some spurs

Variety, like spices
Adventures, held him like vices
A somewhat low boredom threshold
The changes he wrought sometimes classed as bold
But the loves of his life were never over in trices

Two anchors, shuttered and pedaled
Were not just things with which he purely medaled
A continent crossed
And a dream never lost
Maybe those were the things which, to be a writer, would herald

A religious beginning
May have meant not too much sinning
But God lost and Maslow found
Self-actualization, philosophy and psychology led to changes profound
And so, on balance, a route to winning

The game of chess
At ten, did impress
Early lessons in strategy
And sacrificial proclivity
But, maybe, this is to digress

Accountant, recruiter, photographer and writer
Added to these, Mata Ortiz made things even brighter
Where would it end?
And what could transcend
Daughters, husbands, grandchildren - no need to pretend.

2. **Beckoning**   *Life Beckons*

Beckoning

Except for one's final farewell, a new beginning follows every end
A new opportunity on which one's mortal capital to expend
Only once upon this earth, implies you should not let time go to waste
It will be impacted by your decisions and may not be to everyone's taste

You are an individual, and life, your most important possession
It may be challenging, but things worthwhile need to find expression
Regardless of your age, you're an actor on this stage
Rich or poor, how will or can you improve the next page

The treasure, we each seek, varies from person to person
Depending on the input, its value one may enhance or worsen
How can it be measured and would it be worthwhile?
Of course it could be such an approach is not your style

To make the best of every situation can be so rewarding
Even an unmitigated disaster, like a river - fording
There may be no direct correlation between giving and receiving
But, to say there's none lacks perception and is self-deceiving

As you look ahead, seek to eradicate uncertainty and fear
It will help to make your course of action so much more clear
And, as you treat others, as you would like to be treated
You will find you win more often than you are defeated.

Good Luck

Index

Notes:

Contact the Author via: **Twitter**   **@EdwardReLife**

Web Site   **http://www.EdwardReLife.com/**

www.ingramcontent.com/pod-product-compliance
Lightning Source LLC
Chambersburg PA
CBHW080500110426
42742CB00017B/2955